W9-AVZ-729

DEATH IN DECEMBER

'Beautifully written ... The author handles the account
carefully, but nonetheless painfully vividly.'
Evening Echo

'Focuses on the fact that this murder involved a person,
not a statistic. Ample detail and vivid images ... The reader
isn't left feeling short-changed.'
Irish Independent

'An engaging read. Excellent writing.'
Drogheda Independent

'Sheridan peels away each layer of untruth or myth.'
Irish Examiner

MICHAEL SHERIDAN

has combined a career as a journalist with that of theatre director. He has written extensively on the Sophie Toscan du Plantier murder and police investigation. Michael was also the main screenplay writer for the film *When the Sky Falls*, which was based on the life and death of journalist Veronica Guerin.

DEATH
IN DECEMBER

The Story of Sophie Toscan du Plantier

MICHAEL SHERIDAN

THE O'BRIEN PRESS
DUBLIN

First published 2002 by The O'Brien Press Ltd,
20 Victoria Road, Dublin 6, Ireland.
Tel: +353 1 4923333; Fax: +353 1 4922777
E-mail: books@obrien.ie
Website: www.obrien.ie
This edition published 2004

ISBN: 0-86278-893-5

Copyright for text © Michael Sheridan
'The Libel Hearing' text © copyright Ralph Riegel 2004
Copyright for typesetting, layout, editing, design
© The O'Brien Press Ltd

All rights reserved. No part of this publication may be reproduced
or utilised in any form or by any means, electronic or mechanical,
including photocopying, recording or in any information storage and
retrieval system, without permission in writing from the publisher.

British Library Cataloguing-in-Publication Data
Sheridan, Michael, 1947 Oct. 17-
Death in December: the story of Sophie Toscan du Plantier
1.Du Plantier, Sophie Toscan - Death and burial 2.Women - Ireland -
Biography
3.Murder - Investigation - Ireland - Cork
I.Title
364.1'523'092

3 4 5 6 7 8 9 10
04 05 06 07 08 09

Editing, typesetting, layout and design: The O'Brien Press Ltd
Printing: AIT Nørhaven A/S, Denmark

CREDITS

Cover photograph and pictures on pages (i), (ii), (iii), (iv), (v), (vi), (vii), (viii), (ix), (x), (xi)
bottom, (xii) top, (xv) bottom, (xvi) bottom, courtesy of the Bouniol family.
Back cover photograph and pics on pages (xi) top, (xii) bottom, (xiii),
(xiv), (xv) top, (xvi) top by John Minihan.
Excerpt from the personal diaries of Sophie Toscan du Plantier courtesy of the Bouniol
family, reproduced by permission of Daniel Toscan du Plantier; excerpt from 'A Devil In
The Hills', The New Yorker, January 2000, by permission of John Montague and Elizabeth
Wassell; quote from The Thing He Loves by permission of Elizabeth Wassell; 'A Dream of
Death' by WB Yeats is reproduced by permission of AP Watt Ltd,
on behalf of Michael B Yeats.

DEDICATION

This book is dedicated to the memory of

Sophie Toscan du Plantier

28 July 1957 – 23 December 1996

And to her family and extended family who
share with my mother Patsy and her friends
Maxie and Cissie Dooley the essence
of good, which will always triumph over
evil and restore our faith in humanity.

ACKNOWLEDGEMENTS

This story would have been incomplete without the unprecedented co-operation of Sophie's family, Georges, Marguerite and Bertrand Bouniol and Marie Madeleine Opalka. How they and Sophie's son, Pierre Louis, younger brother Stephane and cousins Alexandra and Patricia have survived the grief is beyond my comprehension. My admiration for their courage is unbounded. I am also very grateful for the time, support and co-operation of Daniel Toscan du Plantier.

The book could not have been published without the help of a large number of people, many of who, for professional or personal reasons, prefer to remain anonymous. I am greatly indebted to them for their time, consideration and expertise. I would like to thank the people of Schull who have been unfailingly welcoming during my time there researching the story. Special thanks to Val Duffy, his wife Vera and his staff at the East End Hotel for their generosity and co-operation.

My gratitude also to Bill Hogan, cheesemaker extraordinaire, for his time; to Josephine Hellen, Leo Bolger, John Montague and Elizabeth Wassell, and to master photographer John Minihan for his great company and unerring eye. To Bill Crozier and the committee of the Schull Arts Festival for an inspired opening, and to local historian Michael O'Carroll for his enviable knowledge of centuries of happenings in the area. And to the many other people of the area who wish to remain anonymous.

My thanks to retired DI Gerry O'Carroll for an entrée to a world that previously had been entirely foreign to me, and to his wife Kathleen and daughters Ellie and Mags for providing a stimulating world of love and fun for Cian and Fionn, for which I also owe a big thank you to my daughter Sarah. Thanks to Ger for putting up with the impossible and irritable author and his manifest insecurities. To Marty and Maria for the same over the years. A special thank you to my nephew, Sheridan Flynn, for his assistance.

I am grateful for the continuing support and the commission for the article that inspired this book from Aenghus Fanning, Anne Harris and Willie Kealy of the *Sunday Independent*. I will not forget the support and spiritual assistance of songwriter supreme Jimmy McCarthy, and the wise counsel of Hugh Duffy. And last but not least to the editorial help and wisdom of Mary Webb and Íde ní Laoghaire, all at The O'Brien Press, and Billy Ryan for words of advice and encouragement.

Contents

PROLOGUE

Monday, 23 December 1996

It was just two days after the winter solstice and dawn came late to the valley of Toormore. As the first streaks of colour lightened the sky, the full moon lost its potency and the five-second flash of the Fastnet lighthouse over Roaring Water Bay dimmed.

Lights began to come on in the houses scattered throughout the remote parish in West Cork.

Only forty-eight hours left in the countdown to Christmas Day. Although the townland was outwardly peaceful – sheep grazing unconcernedly on the rough, salt-tanged grass of the sloping fields, the valley still and quiet in the chilly morning air – the sense of excitement and anticipation that precedes the biggest feast day of the year was palpable. In every house the final preparations for a traditional Irish Christmas were fully underway: presents were being wrapped surreptitiously while the children slept, jelly was setting for the trifle, beds were being aired for returning family members. And soon the shops in Schull, Skibbereen and Ballydehob would be open.

Like almost everyone else, Shirley Foster still had things to do for the holiday. Shortly before 10.00am she closed her front door behind her and sat into her car, intending to drive the eight miles to Schull. She eased the car past the neighbouring house, around the S-bend and down the steep, gravel laneway that led into the valley and out onto the main road. As she neared the gate at the bottom of the lane, something caught her eye.

A piece of white material fluttered on the low barbed-wire fence, just inside the open gate. Then she saw the crumpled form lying at the base of the fence. Shirley put her foot on the brake and stopped the car. Her heart racing, she opened the driver's door. There was blood, a lot of blood. She turned and ran back up the laneway to her house.

* * *

The bloody, lifeless body was that of Sophie Toscan du Plantier, a beautiful thirty-nine-year-old Frenchwoman. Sophie was a frequent visitor to the converted farmhouse that she had bought five years earlier as a retreat from her busy life in Paris. In a phone call to her husband the previous night, Sophie had told him that she would be leaving Toormore the following day, 24 December, to return to Paris and spend Christmas with him at their country home in Ambax, near Toulouse.

She never made it home.

She would never celebrate Christmas again.

PART ONE

THE FATEFUL JOURNEY

Chapter One
THE FACTS

Thursday, 19 December 1996

Sophie Toscan du Plantier spent the evening in the fashionable Paris nightclub *Les Bains Douches* in Rue Bourg-l'Abbé with her husband Daniel, a famous and influential French film producer. She had escorted him to the annual Christmas party of Unifrance, the national film promotion board, of which Daniel was chairman. Sophie, too, had worked for Unifrance for some time before becoming an independent television documentary producer, so she knew or had worked with many of the people at the party. She circulated among the guests, but always returned to Daniel's table, which was occupied by a number of well-known actors and the film-maker Alain Terzian. Those she spoke to that night described her as being radiant, vivacious and in good form. She was, however, very tired, having recently returned from a long trip to a film festival in Acapulco and also having just completed a television film for the Arte channel.

While Sophie socialised and chatted to the luminaries of the French film world, her mind was on a location far removed from the glamorous nightlife of Paris. She had decided to spend a few days in her remote holiday home in West Cork.

Sophie had bought the house five years earlier and visited several times a year, always with family or friends. But this time, for the first time, she was making the journey alone. Everyone she had invited to join her had declined. This close to Christmas, they all had other pressing commitments. It was understandable. But in the light of subsequent events, it was a decision her family and friends came to regret bitterly and remains one of those 'if only' thoughts that will haunt them forever.

Friday, 20 December

The morning after the party, Sophie left her apartment in the seventh *arrondissement* of Paris and headed for Charles de Gaulle Airport, where she boarded the 11.30am (Irish time) Aer Lingus flight to Dublin. Flight EI 521 touched down in Dublin at 1.00pm. Passengers travelling on to Cork remained on board and the flight took off again at 1.45pm, arriving at Cork Airport at 2.25pm. Five minutes later, Sophie was recorded on a security video as she wheeled her luggage into the arrivals hall. The footage shows an elegant woman with long blonde hair braided into a single plait that hangs over her right shoulder. She is wearing a three-quarter-length black wool jacket and a green scarf over a polo-neck jumper and grey trousers, with black boots. She looks pale and tired.

She made her way to the Avis desk and picked up the keys to her hired car: a silver Ford Fiesta, registration number 96 C 14459. Cork is a small airport, without the complications and delays inevitable in larger international terminals, so by 2.40pm Sophie was driving the Fiesta out of the airport and turning onto the N71 – the Bandon–Clonakilty–Ballydehob road. It was a route she was by now very familiar with and she made good progress. Most of the cars on the road were local, bearing the 'C' registration that denotes Cork, but already there were a number of cars with Dublin and other county registrations – people who had taken an extra day off in order to avoid the pre-Christmas traffic build-up that comes with the annual migration of city-dwellers back to their rural roots for the holiday.

By 3.30pm Sophie had reached Ballydehob, where she pulled in at the Texaco filling station and bought some household supplies. She set off again, passing through Schull and then on to the last eight miles towards Dunmanus West and the townland of Toormore, where her house is located. By the time she crossed Kilfeadda bridge, six miles beyond Schull, darkness had fallen. There she turned right onto the boreen that led into the valley, twisting and turning for over a mile before reaching the gateway to her house.

At around 4.30pm Sophie drew up before the metal gate that guarded the entrance to the laneway she shared with two other houses. She got out of the car and stopped for a moment to look up at the house, feeling her heart lift as it always did when she returned to her chosen home. She drew back the bolt that anchored the gate to an old, whitewashed pillar and stepped aside as the six-barred gate swung out-wards. Returning to her car, she drove on to the laneway, then went back and closed the gate securely. Sheep grazed the fields surrounding the house and it was an unwritten rule that the gate was always kept closed.

She made her way up the steep, gravelled lane, her head-lights showing where the grass was overgrown in the centre of the driveway. There was very little traffic on the laneway: Shirley Foster and Alfie Lyons were the only year-round residents; the other house, to the right of her own, was also a holiday home, belonging to a family named Richardson. She swung the car left at the top where the laneway curved inwards and parked in her usual spot, facing the blank gable-end wall of her house.

The house was in darkness, so, leaving the car lights on to provide illumination, she walked across to the porch, stepping carefully on the uneven local stone that paved the area around the front of the house. She unlocked the porch door, then the main door and reached in to flick the light switch that controlled both the inside lights and the outside light on the corner of the gable wall. She went back to the car for her luggage and shopping, then returned to the house.

A week before leaving Paris, Sophie had telephoned Mrs Josephine Hellen, the local woman who acted as caretaker of the house in her absence, to alert her to her forthcoming visit. Earlier in the day Josephine Hellen had gone over to the house, turned on the heating and lit the two open fires so that the place would be warm and cosy when Sophie arrived. Josephine had left the house sometime after 2.00pm. As it was still daylight at that time she had not turned on the lights.

As well as the glowing fires, there was another welcoming sight in the house – a surprise. The windowsills and mantelpieces were festooned with freshly picked holly, its serrated, glossy leaves and masses of bright red berries making the room festive and cheerful. Mrs Hellen had decorated the house in the traditional West Cork manner as a Christmas present for its owner. It was a thoughtful, homely gesture and one typical of Josephine Hellen. Sophie was touched.

She went upstairs and into her bedroom. It was simply furnished, her mattress perched on top of an elevated wooden frame that she had had specially constructed so she could see the pulsing flashes from the Fastnet lighthouse through the uncurtained window. She found the winking light comforting. Indeed, the presence of the Fastnet lighthouse was one of the reasons she had been attracted to this house in the first place – standing here, although you couldn't actually hear the crash of the waves as the Atlantic Ocean rolled into Dunmanus Bay, Toormore Bay and Roaring Water Bay, it was easy to imagine the scene. She left her things in the bedroom and went back downstairs.

At 4.45pm the telephone rang. It was Josephine Hellen, checking to make sure that Sophie had arrived and everything was all right. Sophie told her that she was delighted with the preparations and thanked her particularly for the arrangements of holly. She said that she hadn't yet made up her mind which day she would return to Paris, but that she would be spending New Year in Dakar, West Africa, with her husband and their friend, Jerome Clement, head of the Arte channel, along with Clement's sister, Catherine. Mrs Hellen reminded her that there would be no flights out of Cork on Christmas Day, and added that if she did decide to stay on, she would be welcome to join the Hellen family for Christmas dinner. It would not be the only invitation that Sophie would receive during her stay. This was typical of the spirit of West Cork – the door was always open and never more so than at Christmas. At the end of the conversation Sophie promised to phone Josephine later in the evening.

After settling in and having something to eat, Sophie relaxed and read at the wooden table in the small kitchen just off the main living-room. Later, she rang Josephine Hellen back, but as Mrs Hellen was not at home she left a message with her daughter, Catherine, saying that she would phone Mrs Hellen again the following day to make some arrangements.

Although she would have liked to have had company, it didn't really bother Sophie to be on her own. The peace and quiet was welcome. Things had been very hectic for the past while. She had been working hard on her documentary and the trip to Acapulco had been very tiring. She accepted that film festivals were part and parcel of the movie business, but she didn't really enjoy the hype and the artificiality that went with them. A few days away from everyone, with maybe a chance to do some writing, was just what she needed.

At 11.25pm Sophie's best friend, Agnes Thomas, phoned from Paris and they talked for about twenty minutes. Shortly afterwards, exhausted from her journey and feeling the effects of last night's party, Sophie switched off the downstairs lights and headed up the wooden stairs to bed.

Saturday, 21 December
Sophie drove into Schull, left her car in the car park opposite the East End Hotel and walked up the street, stopping at Brosnan's Spar supermarket where she bought some food

and household items. It was just after 3.00pm. The supermarket, like all the other shops, was bright with Christmas decorations, and business was brisk as people stocked up on supplies to last them over the holiday period.

The main street in Schull can be walked in five minutes, from the harbour on the east side to the Allied Irish Bank premises at the top of the hill. During the summer it is often crowded with visitors who use the harbour as a base for sailing and yachting, but in winter things are quiet. The arrival of a stranger would be noticed immediately. As she walked up the street, Sophie received nods and smiles of greeting from locals who recognised the Frenchwoman from her visits over the years.

But one person, a man, noted her presence with more interest than anyone else. He had seen her before, may even have met her, but she was unlikely to remember him. Was she alone, he wondered? He decided to watch her and find out.

Unaware that she had acquired a shadow, Sophie called into the Courtyard Bar, where she had a quick cup of tea, and then browsed for a while in Farrell's, an arts and crafts shop at the top of the town. At 3.25pm she walked across to the bank opposite the shop and withdrew IR£200 from the ATM. Then she made her way back down to the car park and drove home.

The watcher saw her leave Schull, alone. It appeared that

she was on her own. But he would keep an eye out, check around to see if anyone knew for sure.

Sophie's car was seen parked outside her house at 4.15pm and, as far as can be ascertained, she did not leave the house for the rest of the evening.

Sunday, 22 December
Sophie drove from Toormore through Goleen and out towards Mizen Head, on the tip of the peninsula, where she went for a walk. Between 2.00pm and 4.00pm she visited a French-speaking couple, Thomas and Yvonne Ungerer, with whom she had become friendly on one of her previous visits. Strasbourg-born Tomi Ungerer is an internationally acclaimed illustrator and writer, and he and his wife had moved to West Cork in 1975. Their home at Three Castle Head is about ten miles from Sophie's house, in a beautiful spot that looks out over Dunmanus Bay and beyond to Bantry Bay. Sophie drank two glasses of wine with the Ungerers. She was in a good and positive mood, apart from being vague about her plans to return to France.

After she left the Ungerers, she drove to Crookhaven where she called into a waterfront bar and restaurant owned by Billy and Angela O'Sullivan. It was one of her favourite stopping places when out on walks or drives. The couple asked Sophie if she would like to join them for a drink on Christmas Day, but she said that she was not sure whether or not she would be there. She had a cup of tea with the O'Sullivans, then left after about fifteen minutes and drove back to Dunmanus West.

In retrospect, Sophie's reply to the O'Sullivans and her vagueness with the Ungerers regarding her travel arrangements seem strange, as it later transpired that prior to leaving France she had already booked her return flight to Paris. In fact, she held two tickets, one for the following night, 23 December, and the other for Christmas Eve. Although the two bookings indicate some indecision on her part about her actual return date, she had certainly made no arrangements to stay on in West Cork until Christmas Day.

At 5.30pm Sophie rang Agnes Thomas in Paris, and when she got no reply she left a message on the answer phone wishing her friend a happy birthday. Half an hour later a man passing by saw lights on upstairs and downstairs in Sophie's house. At 7.30pm Sophie telephoned Josephine Hellen, but Josephine's daughter, Catherine, told her that her mother was not at home. She then rang a local tradesman, Pat Hegarty, who was also unavailable. At 9.10pm she again rang the Hellens and again spoke to Catherine, as Josephine had still not returned.

At 9.20pm Sophie's neighbour, Shirley Foster, was pulling the curtains before going to bed. She noticed that the outside light on the gable end of Sophie's house was on.

By 9.45pm Josephine Hellen had returned home, and

hearing that Sophie had been looking for her, she rang the house. She spoke with Sophie and they made arrangements to meet at noon the following day. Mrs Hellen had normal business to settle relating to the house, such as the presentation of bills and money to pass on from a pay phone that had been installed. Sophie told her that she had been trying to contact Pat Hegarty, whom she had hired on a previous visit to do some plastering work. She was very happy with the job and wanted him to carry out alterations and renovations to one of the open fireplaces. She asked Mrs Hellen if she would bring Pat with her when she called over the following day. Josephine did contact Pat Hegarty on Sophie's behalf and he said he would make his own way over to Toormore in the afternoon. By that time, of course, news of the tragedy had leaked out and Pat Hegarty never made the journey.

Mrs Hellen says that her memory of their last telephone conversation is that Sophie seemed in great form and that they spent fifteen minutes chatting, and Sophie apologised for the fact that she had not dropped over to see Mrs Hellen since her arrival.

At 11.00pm (midnight, French time) Sophie rang her husband, Daniel, in Paris. He was on another line and could not talk, but he returned her call ten minutes later. It was a long and relaxed conversation between husband and wife, with Sophie portraying no unease or anxiety about being on her own. Daniel would later tell me that his wife could be an enigma, even to him. There were aspects of Sophie that he did not know and which remained a mystery to him throughout their relationship. Sophie teased Daniel for a while, saying she wasn't sure when she would be back, but finally confirmed that she would be returning to Paris on Christmas Eve and the couple made plans to spend Christmas Day at their country home in Ambax. At the time of their telephone conversation, Daniel got the impression that she was either in bed, or preparing to go to bed.

After her conversation with her husband, Sophie retired to bed, bringing with her the book she had been reading in the kitchen. Outside, the temperature had fallen close to zero degrees. She decided not to sleep in her own bedroom that night and chose instead the guest bedroom at the far end of the corridor. Mrs Hellen had prepared this room too because she had been under the impression that Alexandra, Sophie's first cousin, would be accompanying her on the trip to Toormore. The bed was a simple double mattress on the floor, but the room was located just above the kitchen and had the advantage of an electric heater that Sophie could plug in if she got cold during the night.

She read for a little while before going to sleep.

Sophie's chosen bedtime reading was a collection of poems by WB Yeats. The book was found open at the page where she had stopped reading.

The poem was entitled 'A Dream of Death'.

Chapter Two

THE BODY

Monday, 23 December

After Shirley Foster made her gruesome discovery on the morning of 23 December, she abandoned her car and ran up the steep laneway, past Sophie Toscan du Plantier's house and into her own yard. When she got inside her house she was white and shaking with shock. Breathlessly, she told her partner, Alfie Lyons, that she had seen a body by the gate. Alfie immediately set off down the laneway. He came to a halt thirty metres from the body. Although from that distance it would have been hard to identify it, his first thoughts nevertheless were of his French neighbour. He went back up the lane to Sophie's house and banged loudly on the porch door several times. When there was no reply, he returned to his own house and dialled 999.

The emergency call was put through to Bandon Garda Station, which is the Divisional Headquarters for the area. At 10.10am Garda Eugene McCarthy took the call. He listened and made notes as Alfie Lyons told him that he had found a body and gave details of the location. Garda McCarthy then relayed the information to Garda Martin Malone at Schull Garda Station. Sergeant Gerard Prendeville and Garda Billy Byrne were detailed to travel to the scene of the crime. They arrived in a squad car at 10.38am, halted outside the open gate and went to where the body lay.

It was a pitiful and sickening sight. The body lay face upwards on the right-hand side of the laneway, a short distance from the entrance gate. It was clothed in a blood-soaked T-shirt and white leggings. The left leg was splayed out and partially impaled on one of the strands of barbed-wire fencing that ran along the side of the lane. A torn section of the leggings was attached to the barbed wire – it was this that had caught Shirley Foster's attention as she drove down from her house. A navy dressing gown lay beside the body, as though it had been grabbed and pulled off, or else abandoned by the victim in her frantic efforts to get away from her attacker.

There were lacerations all over both arms and hands. One finger had a deep cut and was probably broken. A clump of human hair protruded from a tightly clenched fist. But the eyes of the horrified policemen were drawn irresistibly to the battered face and head. A halo of blood had soaked into the ground around the head, which had sustained horrific injuries of a type that could only have resulted from a ferocious attack with a heavy object. A blood-stained cavity block lying beside the body seemed the most likely murder weapon.

There was also blood on the gate, suggesting that the victim had reached the barrier before being pulled back to her death. Even for the most hardened murder investigators, this would have been a heart-breaking scene.

Sergeant Prendeville contacted Bantry Garda Station for medical and spiritual assistance, while Garda Byrne began the vital task of preserving the scene. He made a written description of everything he could see: the position of the body, the arrangement of the clothes, the presence and condition of the concrete cavity block and any other items around the crime scene. From then on he would also record the names of all visitors to the site. Everyone, except those involved in official procedures, was kept at a safe remove.

At 11.00am Dr L O'Connor from Schull arrived on the scene, examined the body and pronounced the victim dead. He also made detailed written notes about the scene and the injuries he observed. He noted that *rigor mortis* had set in. The doctor left the scene half an hour later. At 11.20am two more cars drew up at the gate, one containing a priest from nearby Goleen, Fr Denis Cashman, who administered the Last Rites, the other bringing Garda Pat Joy from Bantry Garda Station. At half-past midday Josephine Hellen's husband, Finbar, who had known Sophie since 1993, arrived and identified the pitiful remains. The battered rag doll, lying defenceless and open to the humiliation of the public gaze, was indeed the beautiful Frenchwoman whose elegance and charm had impressed all those she had encountered in this remote part of rural Ireland, which, in a terrible irony, she had chosen as a place where she could 'reste sereine'.

The State Pathologist, Dr John Harbison, had been notified of the murder, but was unable to travel to West Cork that day. Until the arrival of Dr Harbison, the body would have to remain undisturbed *in situ*. This was most unfortunate and raised a lot of queries subsequently, but at that time the State Pathologist's office was chronically under-resourced. With murder on the increase in Ireland, including a huge upsurge in drug-related fatalities, it was farcical that only one person was employed in this capacity and required to attend every crime-related death. An Assistant State Pathologist, Dr Marie Cassidy, was appointed soon afterwards, but too late for the matter of the Du Plantier case.

Meanwhile, the Gardaí continued their work at the scene. The Forensics Laboratory in the Phoenix Park, Dublin, had been notified, and that evening a forensics team arrived to join the local Gardaí in Toormore.

The police photographer consulted with detectives and technicians to ascertain what exactly was required to be photographed in detail; the photographic record has to be made before evidence can be collected or moved. The first photographs were taken from several different angles and provided an overview of the crime scene. Then there were mid-range shots of the various components of the crime: the scene, the body, clothing, murder weapon and the patterns of bloodstaining. Finally, each item of evidence was photographed in close-up detail, including, of course, the shocking but vital pictures of the ruined face and the other horrific injuries inflicted on the victim. Then, a blue plastic covering was gently laid over the remains of Sophie Toscan du Plantier.

The team examined the laneway, the adjoining field and the interior of the house, checking for any trace evidence, dusting for fingerprints and collecting samples for later DNA analysis.

All through that day and on into the morning of Christmas Eve, a rota of policemen kept watch over the murdered woman. As households in West Cork readied the candles that would stay alight overnight for the traditional Christmas vigil, this was one vigil that was both unseasonable and unwelcome. For some of the Gardaí present it must have been the saddest duty of their careers.

Back in Paris, Sophie's husband and family were as yet unaware of the terrible tragedy that had befallen them. The Gardaí had informed their French counterparts and there had apparently been attempts to make contact with the family, but as a result of some breakdown in communication the French police had not spoken to the family by the time a French television news bulletin at 8.00pm (local time) carried a report of the murder of a Frenchwoman in an area 100 kilometres from Cork City.

Sophie's mother, Marguerite Bouniol, watched the news bulletin and was immediately overwhelmed by a feeling that the unnamed victim was her daughter. She and her husband, Georges, contacted Marguerite's sister, Marie Madeleine Opalka, who was Sophie's favourite aunt and confidante. Frantic phone calls were made to the house in Dunmanus West, but there was no reply. Later that day, Marie Madeleine's daughter and Sophie's cousin, Alexandra, took on the task of telephoning and contacting anyone she could think of in Ireland who might have news. Eventually, she was put in touch with a member of the investigating team, but he had no authority to confirm the name of the deceased. By this time it was close to 11.00pm (Irish time). Sophie's body had been discovered thirteen hours earlier and her family still did not know.

Finally, Alexandra contacted Josephine Hellen, whom she had met on previous visits to Toormore with Sophie. She pleaded with the caretaker to give her a simple 'yes' or 'no' answer to the question she then put to her: 'Is Sophie alive?'

There was a pause. Then Josephine answered in a choked whisper, 'No.'

Alexandra could not bring herself to ring her mother, so her sister, Patricia, imparted the dreadful news. Marie Madeleine then told Sophie's parents. Daniel Toscan du Plantier was contacted by a member of the family and informed that Sophie had been murdered. The truth was out and the nightmare began to unfold.

Tuesday, 24 December
That morning, the State Pathologist Dr John Harbison arrived at the scene, made a preliminary examination and then supervised the removal of the body. Sophie's remains were placed in a coffin, loaded into a hearse and taken on the seventy-four-mile journey to Cork City. Dr Harbison followed in his car. Just after lunchtime, the hearse arrived at Cork University Hospital and the coffin was brought to the morgue. The body was removed and placed on a stainless-steel table in preparation for the post-mortem, which began at approximately 2.00pm. The results of this post-mortem were revealed by coroner Dr Colm Quigley at a preliminary inquest held in Bantry on 17 April 1997. Dr Harbison testified that his examination had determined that Sophie Toscan du Plantier had died from a fractured skull and blunt-instrument trauma. As in all cases where a death is still under criminal investigation, the inquest was

adjourned pending the resolution of the murder enquiries.

In Paris, Sophie's distraught parents, Georges and Marguerite, along with her brother Bertrand and Marie Madeleine Opalka, boarded a flight to Cork. Then they made the dreaded trip to Cork University Hospital. Bertrand was the first to go into the morgue. When he came out he was visibly shocked.

'That's not Sophie,' he said quietly. What he meant was that the ruined face he had just seen bore no resemblance to his stunningly beautiful sister.

The other family members then went into the morgue. Marguerite recognised only her daughter's perfectly shaped nose, the one part of her face that had escaped the brutality of the attack. She asked to see Sophie's hands, but was dissuaded. The killer, in his rage, had broken some of her fingers and inflicted one very deep wound.

Daniel Toscan du Plantier did not come to Ireland to see his wife's body. In explanation he told me, 'I knew the extent of Sophie's injuries from conversations with the police and I could not bear to have remembered her as anything but the beautiful, vibrant woman that I knew and loved. I would have been haunted by the mutilation of her face and it would have obliterated the wonderful memories of her smiles.'

Deeply distressed, he retreated to his country home in Ambax, where he made arrangements for the funeral and burial.

The Bouniols and Marie Madeleine returned to Paris on St Stephen's Day, 26 December. On 27 December Sophie's body was taken from Cork to Dublin and then flown to Paris, from where it was transferred to Toulouse on 28 December. After an overnight vigil near Columiéres, Sophie was finally laid to rest in the small local cemetery, not far from the house in Ambax where she had spent so many happy hours.

Chapter Three

THE MURDER –
A Fictionalised Reconstruction

On the night of Sunday, 22 December 1996 Sophie Toscan du Plantier sat reading at her kitchen table, her chair set close to the radiator for warmth, another chair pulled up so that she could rest her feet on it. Occasionally she dipped into the bowl of olives on the table, but a bottle of champagne remained unopened. Champagne is for drinking with friends and she was not expecting any visitors. Soon, she would go upstairs to bed, but for now she was happy to enjoy the peace and quiet of her cosy kitchen, her mind free from the hectic pace of last week's activities.

* * *

Eight miles away, in Schull, a man joined with the Sunday night crowds enjoying their weekend drinks in a local pub. The pre-Christmas spirit had taken hold and 'rounds' were being bought with more generosity than was perhaps normal. It was a time for rejoicing and celebrating, particularly in a small and scattered community often isolated by the vagaries of winter, unlike in the summer months when the town would be bursting at the seams with the sailing crowd. But although the man mingled and drank with friends and acquaintances, his mind was already elsewhere and an idea of what he would do later on was taking hold in his head. And he *could* do it.

The seed had been planted when he had spotted her on her own in Schull on Saturday. He had watched her go into the Courtyard Bar; he had even considered following her in, but thought better of it. He would just hang around. It only seemed like minutes when she emerged again and went into Farrell's shop. Plenty of money and nothing to do with it, he thought bitterly. The house must be worth a fortune now. Half the houses in the area were owned by people like her – able to afford to keep a second or third house empty most of the time – while he was strugging to keep any roof over his head. She came out of the shop and he saw her withdraw a wad of cash from the ATM before heading back to her hired car. It was a long time since he had had any real money. Resentment coursed through him.

He had watched her comings and goings since Saturday, and was now certain that there was no one with her. On all the other visits there had been companions, older people – maybe parents – and sometimes kids who could have got in the way. But not this time.

He was on a high. He needed to be the centre of

attention. He often had grandiose ideas and plans. Usually they came to nothing in the end. He smiled to himself, wondering what they would say if they knew what he was thinking now. The conversation had veered away from him and he hated that. He got the distinct feeling that he was being talked about. Not in a complimentary way. Well, they might be talking about him outside the pub sooner than they knew.

He knew that he could make his way up the hill overlooking the valley on foot. And this night luck was on his side in the form of Mother Nature. There was a bright full moon and a clear sky, which would make the countryside perfectly visible. Almost as good as daylight. The Fates were with him.

He knew just how he would make his approach. Then, once he reached the house, he would knock on the back door. He would try to get himself invited inside. He would control this cool, sophisticated woman who fancied herself as an artist and a person of substance. He thought of her windswept blonde hair and the haughty way she held her head. She had hips like a boy. He liked that in a woman. Bigger women put him off sexually – too maternal.

Everything about this woman spelled class and mocked his own inadequacies. He had heard that she was a writer and a television producer. And on top of all that, she was married to some big shot in the film industry. She probably didn't have to work at all if she didn't want to. Just doing it for the 'artistic satisfaction'. And here he was with talent to burn, and who recognised it? Nobody.

He could feel his blood beginning to boil. All her money and power would be no use to her when her blood was spilling and she screamed for mercy. Why did these stupid women have to provoke him to violence? Why couldn't women just do as they were told and shut up? But no, they were always trying to prove who was running the show.

The only difference between this Frenchwoman and him was luck and connections. That's all. He could reduce that luck and those connections to nothing. And then he would be someone; someone to be admired or feared, he didn't care which. It was all the same, really.

He felt very confident tonight, a sense of destiny about to be fulfilled. As drink fired his intent to boiling point, he watched the clock in the bar creep towards closing time. It seemed to take forever, but he wasn't stupid; leaving early would just make him stand out, and this was one night when he had to be invisible.

* * *

Around 10.40pm Sophie turned off the lights in the kitchen and went to the living-room, bringing her book with her. Sitting on the first step of the open staircase, she partly unlaced her black boots, slipped out of them and left them at the bottom of the stairs, as she always did. She turned off the living-room light and climbed the eleven steps to the landing. She stopped briefly in her own bedroom to watch the pulsing flash of the Fastnet lighthouse. This was like a nightly prayer before the curtain of sleep drew over her.

In the guest bedroom at the end of the corridor she changed into her nightclothes: a T-shirt and leggings. In the bathroom she looked at her face in the mirror. Some of the tiredness had gone out of her eyes. She had been right to make this visit.

She returned to the guest bedroom and got into bed. Settling herself into a comfortable position, she picked up her book. Poetry spoke to her soul, calmed her when she was tired or frustrated. She had written many poems herself, some of them right here in this house. She shivered. The night had turned very cold. Still, she would have plenty of heat soon when she went to Dakar for the New Year. That reminded her. She must ring Daniel. The cordless phone was on the floor beside the bed. She dialled the Paris number. Daniel was on the other line; he would ring back.

At ten minutes past midnight (French time), Daniel returned her call and they chatted for almost an hour. He was happy that she had finally made up her mind about her return flight; she would be home on Tuesday. It would be good to spend Christmas at Ambax, although she would miss her son, Pierre Louis, who was staying with his father for the holiday.

When she put down the phone, Sophie continued to read for a little while. Then tiredness overcame her and she settled down to sleep.

The book lay open on the bed: a collection of work by WB Yeats. He had become a firm favourite of hers. The poem on which Sophie had fallen asleep was from *The Rose* collection: 'A Dream of Death', in which Yeats dreams of his loved one dying in a strange land, far from home and with no friends or family around her. The original title of the poem was 'An Epitaph'. As she slept peacefully in her bed, Sophie could not have imagined how soon the poetic dream would become a nightmarish reality.

* * *

At the time that Sophie was finishing her telephone conversation with her husband, the last stragglers were being cleared from the pub in Schull. The man drove off. The chill in the air had got bitter, but the sky was cloudless. Some miles outside the village he stopped the car on a hill, a suitably elevated spot with a good view of the surrounding countryside and the sea. With the benefit of the moonlight he could see the white shape of Sophie's house, lying just two miles away to the west. He thought again about her body and he was consumed with lust. Something awful, something wonderful was going to happen. He had the power.

He stayed a few minutes more, exulting in the feeling. He drove on home and went to bed for half an hour, then got up, put on a jumper and a heavy jacket and slipped out into the backyard of his house. It was well after 1.30am. He got back into his car and drove in the direction of Dunmanus West. Some distance from Sophie's house, he stopped the car. He would walk from here. On foot, he could merge invisibly into the landscape. Guided by the full moon and the clear sky, he made his way along the roads and boreens, taking short cuts across fields and rocky ground. Once or twice he stumbled; he shouldn't have had so much to drink, but the cold soon began to dissipate the alcohol fumes.

His mind was focused on the woman. He would have her, whether she wanted it or not. And afterwards? His thoughts didn't take him that far. They were on the moment of conquest, the thrill, the feeling of being all-powerful that he loved. He had experienced it before. It was like an addiction, and this time was going to be the biggest rush. He just knew it.

Nothing stirred in the countryside. There was not a sight of another human being. He was an animal on the hunt.

As he rounded a bend he heard the running water of the small river under Kilfeadda bridge. He stopped on the bridge and listened. He looked up towards the rocky ridge in the distance where the Frenchwoman's house was located. He turned right onto the boreen that led to the valley. Another mile and a bit and he would be there.

He was not as fit as he used to be. Not so long ago, ten years maybe, he could have run up the incline without a problem. He had once prided himself on his fitness, but it was gone. He was still strong, but no longer fast. The promise of his youth had disappeared in a puff of nothing. But he was still somebody and he would prove it.

Anticipation carried him on until he reached the gate at the bottom of the laneway. He looked up. The house was in darkness, except for an outside light at the gable end. Everything was quiet. Pulling the sleeve of his jacket down over his hand, he opened the gate and began the steep climb up to the house. The hired car he had seen her driving around Schull was parked at the top of the lane, opposite the gable end of the house. Keeping close to the wall, he edged his way around the house.

It would be easier to go straight to the porch door, but she would be able to see him from the living-room once the light was turned on. She could speak to him through the glass without opening the porch door. He wasn't that stupid.

At the far side of the house he came upon another door. He banged hard on the door, the sound of his knuckles very loud in the stillness of the night. He waited in a fever of impatience. What was keeping her? She should be down by now. He knocked again, hard and sharp.

Upstairs, Sophie woke from her sleep. She heard the staccato rapping on the door. Who could be knocking at this hour? It sounded urgent. Perhaps there was an emergency. The Richardsons were away, so it had to be Shirley, or Alfie.

She pulled back the bed sheets and struggled into her navy dressing gown. Opening the bedroom door, she made her way down the corridor, the flooring cold under her bare feet. Her boots were at the bottom of the stairs, still half-laced. She was able to slip them on without untying the laces. She turned on the living-room light.

There was more banging. And it was coming from the back door, the one nearest Alfie and Shirley's house. Maybe one of them had been taken ill? She was too tired to think straight. She crossed the living-room and went into the kitchen, where she switched on the light.

Sophie looked out the kitchen window but could see no one. She walked through into the pantry and opened the back door. There was nobody there. For the first time she felt a shiver of apprehension. Then a man stepped out from the shadows. A big man; a stranger. Maybe she knew the face? Had she seen him before, around Schull? What on earth was he doing here, at this time of night? He smiled at her and apologised.

He looked wild-eyed and dishevelled. He was breathing heavily and the sour smell of alcohol enveloped her. With dawning horror, Sophie remembered that she was alone in the house. There was no one to call to for help. She was paralysed by fear. The man was saying something. Mumbling. She didn't understand. What did he want? What did he want?

Suddenly he moved towards her, his hand reaching for her. She pushed him away, desperately trying to shut the door with her other hand.

For the man in the doorway this was a signal to unleash all the rage that had been festering inside him. How dare this woman reject him, push him away! He'd teach her. He put his shoulder to the door, forcing it back, and grabbed her by the front of her dressing gown. He pulled her out onto the stone patio. He struck the first blow and felt a rush of pleasure and power as Sophie gasped in pain and surprise.

'Please,' she said, 'why are you doing this?'

He answered her with more blows, his clenched fist catching her again and again. A hatchet stood in a container by the door, probably for chopping logs. He bent to pick it up and she ran.

Sophie was engulfed in a wave of panic and fear. She knew now that she was in mortal danger. There was no reasoning with this man. She ran around the side of the house and towards the field, squeezing through the space between the stone wall and the fence. She had gained a little time; the attacker was having difficulty getting his bulk through the small gap. But her relief was cut short as a searing pain shot through her brain from the impact of the weapon he had managed to swing at her with his long reach.

She stumbled forward, crying, and fell. She felt the blood beginning to stream down from the wound in her head. Dazed, she struggled to her feet and ran on, her boots slipping on the frosty grass. Behind her she could hear him following, crashing through the fuchsias and wild bushes. Briars plucked at her clothes and tore her hands as she blindly grasped the branches, trying desperately to keep her balance on the steep and stony field that fell away down towards the gate. Somewhere in her head she knew that it was all in vain. There was no hope, no rescue out there for her. She was getting further and further away from the only neighbours who could have come to her aid.

Her pursuer was in no rush. Where was she going to go? Beyond the gate there was just the long road through the valley. He was in command here. He increased his pace, and with his long strides he made up the distance the bitch had put between them.

She was at the gate when he caught up with her, trying to open the bar. She heard his footsteps and turned, pleading for mercy. He drew back the hatchet and struck her twice. She tried to parry his blows with her hands but the force of the blows cut into her arms and broke her fingers. Panicked, she turned away from the gate and ran straight at the barbed-wire fence by the side of the lane. She was trying to scramble over it when he pulled her back. He heard the sound of fabric tearing on the barbed spikes as he dragged her out and threw her on the ground. Her hands went about her head for protection, elbows tucked into her chest. She dug her fingers into her hair, shielding her face, her eyes, seeking some kind of purchase that he would be unable to break.

As she lay on the ground he brought the weapon down on her body. Her arm shot forward convulsively, taking with it a hank of her hair that she had pulled out by the roots.

A mile across the valley a man was awoken by a blood-curdling scream like that of a trapped animal.

It was easy after that. He hit her again and again until she stopped struggling. She was unconscious, her life blood draining away from fatal wounds to her head. But her face was still beautiful, dignified. She still looked better than him, superior to him. He was sick with disappointment. This was not the way it was meant to be.

He remembered the pile of concrete blocks he had run past as he emerged from the field and onto the laneway. One of those would sort her out. He bent over the body and placed the head on a small mound of earth. Then he walked over and picked up one of the blocks. It was heavy. He placed the block near her head, then, dropping to his knees, he picked it up in both hands, raised it as high as he could, and brought it crashing down on her skull.

For a little while afterwards he just knelt there, his chest heaving, an unbearable pressure in his ears and head. Then he lifted the block to see the results of his handiwork. Satisfied at last, he dropped the block beside her, by her hip. It was over. He looked down at the woman. She was dead, there was no doubt about that.

He got to his feet. Slowly, reality returned. His clothes were soaked in blood. What had he done? This time he had gone too far.

He looked around him. No one for miles. No witnesses. No nosy neighbours. He looked back up towards the house. Had he left anything incriminating there? There were lights on. That might be noticed.

He would have to calm down. There was nothing to connect him to her. Who would suspect him? Nobody. But it might be better if they had *someone* to suspect. A scapegoat. He would need to create a scenario. He walked up to the house. Luckily, the back door had not swung shut. He took off his shoes before going inside.

He had a good look around the kitchen. It was the first time he had been in the house. It was a lot different than he had imagined. He had assumed that it would be luxurious, but no, it was a simple set-up. He was a bit disappointed. He noticed the chairs pulled together at the wooden table, the bowl of olives and the bottle of champagne. That was good. It made it look like she had company.

He used his elbow to nudge off the light switches. Then he went out the rear door and pulled it shut behind him, the sleeve of his jacket covering his fingers.

When he reached the gate at the bottom of the laneway he picked up the hatchet. He would have to get rid of it. The concrete block was a different matter; it was too heavy to carry any distance. But most of the evidence was on his clothes and he would deal with that quickly enough.

He worried that he might have left traces of blood on the bushes in the field, on the barbed wire or the briars, but there was nothing he could do about that now. And there was so much of her blood around that they might find it impossible to distinguish. One way or another he would just have to brazen it out.

He ran back down the boreen. He was overwhelmed by a sense of achievement. If he could get away with this, all the disappointments of his life – and there were many – would be wiped away like words erased from a blackboard.

First he had to dispose of the hatchet – his fingerprints were all over it. But that shouldn't be a problem. He was surrounded by hundreds of acres of scrubland, full of thickets and boggy holes. Even if you knew what you were looking for, it could take years to find anything hidden out there.

When he had accomplished this task he walked on until he was back at Kilfeadda bridge. He eased himself down a small embankment, took off his boots and began to wash off the blood. He put the boots back on and stood in the water, letting the flow of the stream wash away any residues.

The water in front of him was suddenly illuminated as a car turned off the wide bend and drove slowly over the bridge. For a moment he felt a wave of panic, but it vanished as the car reached the other end of the bridge and disappeared behind the hedgerow and trees. Probably some drunk on his way home. Won't remember a thing.

He climbed back up the embankment and walked on. In the distance he noticed a car parked by the side of the road. He decided to go through the field to avoid being seen. Finally, he reached his own car.

By now it was after 3.30am. As he neared home, exhaustion finally hit him. He had to destroy his bloodstained clothes, but not right now. He needed to lie down and sleep.

First he went into the bathroom. He undressed and dumped the clothes into the bath. He filled it up with cold water, pushing the bulky jacket down until it was completetly submerged. Almost immediately the water turned a dark red. He pulled the plug and filled the bath again and again.

* * *

Back in the laneway in Toormore, Sophie lay, unseen and unseeing, past all pain now.

It was the death of innocence in West Cork.

Chapter Four

THE AFTERMATH –
Rumours and Reactions

The brutal murder of Sophie Toscan du Plantier sent shock waves around the tranquil West Cork communities of Toormore, Schull and Dunmanus West. Josephine Hellen encapsulated the reaction of the entire area when she said to me, 'Nothing like this had ever happened anyone around this beautiful countryside. It ruined everything.'

To understand the depth of the residents' revulsion, it is necessary to understand a little about the people of West Cork, and of the Schull area in particular. The region is known not just for the beauty of the landscape but for the hospitality it has extended over the years to both casual visitors and those who chose to make a second home there, as Sophie had done. In modern times there has been an influx of foreigners into the area, joining the merchant princes of Cork who have traditionally kept holiday homes in West Cork, where they find refuge from the pressures of commerce. Hollywood notables, such as actors Jeremy Irons and Terence Stamp, producer David Puttnam and director Neil Jordan, have substantial properties in the area. A great many artists and poets of various nationalities live and work here, taking inspiration from the scenery and the ambience.

Holiday-makers who discover West Cork are incredibly loyal to the area and return to the same parts for years and sometimes decades, bringing new generations with them to continue the family tradition. The eclectic mix of 'summer people', all-year-rounders and locals get along well, and while newcomers may often be referred to as 'blow-ins', it is a harmless and rather affectionate term. This is a place where violence is neither commonplace nor acceptable. The local people are hard-working, decent and honest. They took this dreadful crime as a personal affront to their reputation, a betrayal of the trust a guest had placed in them and their country.

The killing struck terror into the heart of the rural community. Doors that had always been 'on the latch' were now shut and bolted. A number of women living alone sold their properties and left the area.

The hearts of the people bled for Sophie and her relatives, but also for themselves. And because the victim was French, the word spread far beyond these shores. A horde of international as well as national press crews arrived. An area that had long been associated with beauty, generosity and hospitality was now portrayed as a wild, savage place where an innocent woman was not safe – and where a crazed murderer was able to walk about freely.

Murder in a small community such as this gives rise to a tangled web of suspicion, rumour and counter-rumour. The anonymity bestowed by the concrete jungle of the big city is entirely absent in a rural community where everyone knows everyone else and, more often than not, their private business. The nature of a murder investigation, especially in the initial stages when no one is ruled out as a suspect, inevitably uncovers information about individual members of the community that they would rather keep quiet. Skeletons are taken out of the cupboard and rattled.

And, of course, the media has deadlines to meet and column inches to fill. In the rush to print and obtain 'exclusives', facts are often mangled. The investigators must tread a thin line between needing the public's help and avoiding revealing too much about the case. But the vacuum of information has to be filled, and it can sometimes be hard to differentiate between truth and fiction.

After the brutal slaying of Sophie, myths were created which were bandied around as fact for a number of years. One of the myths that is repeated to this day is that Sophie knew her killer and was having a relationship with him. This has been said to me on several occasions since the murder, the last time as recently as the summer of 2002. This theory was backed up by 'clues' supposedly found by the investigating team. These were:

• two empty, washed wineglasses on the sink in the kitchen. From this it was inferred that Sophie knew her killer well enough to invite him in for a drink late at night. There was not one scintilla of truth in this, as no such wine glasses were found, but it was widely believed and carried as fact by many newspapers at the time.

• the two kitchen chairs. These had been pulled close together, and they were presented as evidence that a cosy, intimate *tête-à-tête* had taken place. The detail about the position of the chairs was true, but the reason they were pulled together was far more practical and prosaic, as I was to discover later. Sophie's mother told me that it was her daughter's habit, when reading, to pull two chairs together so she could sit on one and rest her legs on the other. It was as simple as that.

The implication of an illicit relationship bolstered the other prevalent theory: Sophie was planning to divorce her husband, Daniel, and was in Ireland to think through her decision. This particular suggestion gained widespread credence and was reported in both Irish and French newspapers. In this context, much was made of the circumstances of Sophie's final visit to Toormore. At Christmas time, a time of togetherness, when most people are making their way home to reunions with family and friends, why would a wife leave her husband and home for such a short visit? What was the explanation for Sophie's apparent uncertainty about her return to Paris? Why had she booked *two* separate return flights? And was there some reason why she had come alone – the only time she had ever done so since she had bought the house?

The divorce theory was strengthened by the known facts that Daniel and Sophie had separated for a period in the past and that she had had an extra-marital relationship with another man. Gossip had it that this man had visited the house in Toormore on three occasions, but that wasn't true. To lend further weight to the 'troubled marriage' story, another report suggested that Daniel had spoken to his wife twice on the evening of 22 December and that as a result of what transpired between them, Sophie had decided to leave Ireland as soon as possible – the very next day. This story was intended to give the impression that there was a sudden crisis in the relationship that was forcing Sophie to rush to the airport on the following day, Monday, 23 December. What the gossip mongers did not know was that, although they had had their problems in the past, Daniel and Sophie were enjoying the happiest and most trouble-free period of their relationship.

On the ground, the rumours became more outlandish. One false suggestion was that Daniel, fearing that a divorce would result in Sophie acquiring half his estate, had com-missioned an assassin who deliberately made the killing look like an act of a madman, and not that of a professional hitman, in order to throw investigators off the scent. This is clearly preposterous. Daniel Toscan du Plantier is a man who had been twice divorced before he married Sophie, and although his marriages failed, he maintains regular contact and gets on well with both ex-wives, Marie Christine Barrault and Francesca Comencini.

Supposing, outrageously, that it was a contract killing, the last thing anyone would do would be to send a stranger to Schull, into an area where he would stand out and could be easily identified by witnesses and airport CCTV, and ultimately create a trail that would lead straight back to the organiser. Most assassinations are carried out in a cold and calculated manner and involve long and detailed planning. The manner of Sophie's murder, however, was the act of a savage man out of control and not that of a professional killer.

Such reports caused not only unjustified damage to Sophie's reputation and that of her husband but also huge distress to her grieving family. As a result, the family members agreed a pact of silence in relation to the media.

Another story that was broadcast locally concerned a young foreign man who had been living in the area, but who became depressed after a break-up with his girlfriend and returned home. Some time later he committed suicide and left a note saying that he had done 'something awful', the inference being that he was referring to the murder of Sophie. This was a base, thoughtless and cruel use of a young man's tragic end, thought up but not thought out by someone desperate to explain Sophie's murder. Assuming that the young man did write a farewell note claiming that he had done 'something awful', there was no reason, seeing as he was about to die, to prevent him saying what that awful thing was. It obviously referred to the tragic course of action he was about to take. It was later reported that the allegation of involvement by this young man was 'a claim which the Gardaí said has no foundation and which caused great distress to the man's family.'

* * *

A selection of some of the newspaper reports from the period immediately after Sophie's murder and since give some indication of the reportage of the crime.

On 27 December 1996 the *Irish Independent* described Sophie as 'the estranged wife of noted French film producer Daniel Toscan du Plantier.'

As early as 28 December 1996, only five days after the murder, the *Star*'s front-page banner headline was: 'Murdered Sophie's Tangled Love Life'. Inside, the report indicated that the murdered woman had planned to divorce her second husband and return to her first. It also suggested that Sophie had 'brought a number of male companions to the

West Cork holiday home'. A subsequent *Star* front page was headlined, 'Sophie's Date With Death'.

The *Irish Independent* of 11 January 1997 referred to the 'speculation about Sophie du Plantier's love life' and reported the claim that Sophie intended to leave her second husband and return to her first husband and that she was involved with a third Frenchman.

Also in January 1997, the *Star* carried a story that the killer's fingerprints might have been left on wineglasses in Sophie's cottage.

The French magazine *Paris Match* repeated the wineglass story, saying that two freshly washed glasses had been found on the draining board by the sink. The article also carried a report that a poker wasn't in its usual location by the fireplace in the house, and that at this time of the year, it was the kind of thing whose absence would be noticed immediately.

The *Tribune* magazine of 21 December 1997 also carried the wineglass story, reporting that 'two chairs had been pulled over to a radiator, and two rinsed wineglasses stood by the sink.'

In December 1997 an article in the *Sunday Independent* added a further dimension to this: 'Two chairs were pulled up to a radiator and two wineglasses – one with traces of wine still inside – were found on the mantelpiece and draining board, leading Gardaí to believe she'd had company.'

A *Paris Match* article on police progress in the case

reported: 'It seemed that Sophie had opened the door, without any anxiety, to someone whom she knew. The idea of the killer being a vagrant wandering the locality was dismissed because of the isolation of the area. So the police were also checking the list of passengers who had come through the airports and ports. Had someone known to Sophie come to Dunmanus to kill her?'

As late as 20 January 2002, *The Observer* referred to Sophie as Daniel's 'beautiful but troubled wife'.

* * *

The murder and all the events thereafter have had a lasting effect on the area and its inhabitants, as I discovered. During June 2002, I spent some time in Schull. I was hoping to gain access to the house where Sophie had lived, but I also wanted to talk to people who had known Sophie, to find out what she was like and to get a real sense of the local reaction to her murder. I soon discovered that permission for a visit to the house was unlikely; people were very suspicious of journalists because of the behaviour of those who had, in the course of their duty, tramped all over the area, asked difficult questions and then disappeared when there was little currency left in the story.

I understand their behaviour because that is the nature of the job. News is only news while it is 'hot'. There is always some other story beckoning. Even the most appalling murders can become one- or two-month wonders, revisited over the years if unsolved, but quickly losing the cachet to attract banner headlines and prominent page position. While the stories of serial killings, such as the Moors murders, the Nielsen murders and the Fred and Rosemary West murders, will run and run, almost in soap opera fashion, the unsolved individual killing is subject to the laws of diminishing media returns. The murder of Sophie Toscan du Plantier has been revisited every year on the anniversary of her death, but there is little more to write. Accounts go over the same ground. Six years on, the case is receiving less and less coverage. Unless the killer is apprehended, the likelihood is that very soon it will fade into folk memory, the only reminder being the annual Bouniol family Mass in the church at Goleen. This ceremony emphasises the extent of the tragedy, not just for the grieving relatives, but also for the people of this beautiful part of West Cork.

The stain of Sophie Toscan du Plantier's murder will blot this landscape for as long as the killer walks free and remains unpunished. What award-winning writer and poet John Montague, who lives just a few miles from Schull, describes as a 'poisonous atmosphere' permeated the land in the aftermath of the killing. That atmosphere can still be felt, because through all the years since 23 December 1996, the killer must have continued to live in West Cork; to this day investigators are not looking for anybody outside the region, or in any other part of the country. He has chosen to live as if nothing ever happened.

It is the dual burden of the unsolved murder and the presumption that the killer is still in their midst that makes it impossible for the family and the local people to pray, grieve and get on with their lives. They do not have the small comfort afforded by justice and retribution. The fact that the killer remains unpunished exacerbates the pain.

* * *

The person who knew Sophie best in the locality is Josephine Hellen, and she told me how Sophie had blended in with the community in West Cork and described the impact the murder had had on those living in the area.

Josephine Hellen lives with her husband, Finbar, and their four children, Kay (Catherine), John, Martina and young Siobhán, just a mile away from the house in Toormore. In her capacity as caretaker for the house, Josephine had the most contact with Sophie. Whatever Sophie required, Josephine would provide for her, but they also enjoyed a very good relationship outside the normal employer/employee boundaries.

'Sophie was always, as long as I knew her, which was five years before her death, a perfect lady in all her dealings,' Josephine told me. 'She was mannerly and fair and honest. She would often call over to our house, unannounced, for a cup of coffee and a chat. When her son, Pierre Louis, was younger, he and his cousins would come over and play with our kids. They were fascinated with the animals and they particularly loved the newborn lambs. Sophie loved coming here [to West Cork] as often as she could manage. She would always give me a week's notice so that I could make the house comfortable and I was always welcome there as much as she was welcome in our home.

'Sophie was gracious and thankful for everything that was done for her. That was her nature. She was a joy to deal with, and generous. Sometimes she would only make up her mind to come a short time in advance and not every visit was planned in advance. That was true of Christmas 1996. I had been in contact with Sophie some time before that, because there had been a problem with the heating and the boiler needed to be repaired. While we were discussing it, she said that she was thinking about coming over, but would confirm it later. I was always under the impression that she would be coming over with somebody. I think that was her intention.

'I got a heating repairman from Bantry and he fixed the problem and repaired the boiler. That was more than a week before Sophie arrived. She rang me about that time and told me that she was coming over and would be arriving on either Thursday, 19 December, or Friday, 20 December. She did not discuss when she would be returning, but that was nothing unusual, I was well used to those sorts of arrangements. Again I was under the impression, right to the last minute, that Sophie would not be alone, which is why I prepared the guest room as well as Sophie's room and the rest of the downstairs.'

From the time that Sophie arrived on Friday, 20 December, Josephine found nothing in their communications that was out of the ordinary. Although they had a very good working relationship and indeed friendship, it was only on a rare occasion that Sophie would share confidences. One such occasion had occurred a year or two before (Josephine could not be clear on the exact time), in the summer. Sophie had spoken to Josephine about her desire to have another child.

As far as Josephine could see that fateful Christmas, things had settled down in Sophie's personal life: she seemed happy and in good spirits. She was planning more work on the interior of the house. Their final arrangement regarding the house was that Mrs Hellen would call over at noon on Monday, 23 December. Reliable as always, Josephine set out for the house at the appointed time, with absolutely no prior knowledge of the tragic events that had taken place that morning. She arrived almost simultaneously with her husband, Finbar, who was in the area doing some farm work.

'The place was crawling with police. I could not believe it. I thought there might have been an accident. Murder

Four-year-old Sophie (*right*) with her brother Bertrand and mother Marguerite on holiday in Spain.

Sophie after her First Holy Communion ceremony outside Notre Dame Cathedral with her cousin Alexandra (*left*), aunt Marie Madeleine Opalka, Bertrand (*partly hidden*) and cousin Patricia.

Left: Sophie as a blonde, freckled teenager.

Below: Mother and daughter – Marguerite Bouniol with Sophie.

The radiant bride: a stunning Sophie on her wedding day in 1980.

Above: Sophie, Georges and Marguerite at her wedding in 1980.
Below: Sophie and her first husband, Pierre, in happier times.

Above: Mother and Son – a touching portrait of Sophie and Pierre Louis at three years of age.

Left: The family gathers outside Notre Dame Cathedral after the First Holy Communion of Sophie's younger brother Stephane in 1985.
(from left) Georges, Marguerite, Pierre Louis, Stephane, Sophie and Marie Madeleine Opalka.

Left: Sophie displays her sense of style at a family event in 1987.

Below: Growing up – Pierre Louis, aged nine, shows his affection for his mother.

Left: Sophie and Daniel Toscan du Plantier confirm their wedding vows in Paris in 1990.

Below: Sophie and Daniel at a dinner party in Paris.

Above: Sophie at her writing table in the garden of the country house in Ambax.
Below: Stephane (*left*), Sophie and Bertrand at a family dinner.

never entered my mind and I was in a state of utter shock when one of the Gardaí said that the death was suspicious. Even though I always advised Sophie to keep the front and rear doors locked, it was only a precaution. I never imagined that she would come to any harm. I was utterly devastated. Nothing like this had ever happened anyone around this beautiful countryside. It ruined everything. Nothing will ever be the same again until the murderer is brought to justice.'

The following afternoon – Tuesday, 24 December – Josephine was brought inside the house by detectives who were anxious to see if the caretaker noticed anything unusual about the interior, particularly the kitchen and living-room areas. As far as Josephine could see, there was nothing out of order since she had last been in the house, on the previous Friday afternoon. Most significantly, and despite widespread reports in the media to the contrary, Mrs Hellen did not notice, or mention, anything about a poker missing from its usual place by the fireside. Nonetheless, the so-called fact that a poker was missing gained widespread currency in the media, the inference being that the poker was the first weapon employed in the murder.

Josephine told me that she spent the next six to eight weeks in a constant state of terror. She did not sleep at all in that period of time. To this day she still has a fear of leaving her house and will not stay at home on her own. When she drives down the road past Sophie's house – the route that the killer would have taken – it still sends shivers down her spine. Like the rest of the community, Josephine Hellen will never have peace until Sophie's brutal murder is resolved and her killer pays the price.

Val Duffy, the well-known *maître d'* of the East End Hotel in Schull, confirmed the fact that the murder of Sophie Toscan du Plantier is an agonising burden for the local community to bear.

'Sophie was so well liked in the area. She was a woman of substance, style and culture. On the several times I encountered her over the period of time that she visited Schull, I was highly impressed by her dignity and gentle manner and always by how striking she looked. Her dress, demeanour and looks made her stand out here – and I imagine anywhere she went she had that effect.

'Her murder has certainly cast a shadow over Schull, which she regularly visited to shop at the supermarket or browse around the shops or galleries. And she always popped into the Courtyard Bar for a refreshment and a chat with the owners. The vast majority of people here are decent and hard-working. Our fervent hope is that the killer will be brought to justice. Until this happens there will always be a cloud over Schull.'

Sophie was equally highly regarded by one of the organic cheesemakers in the Schull area, Bill Hogan, an American now resident in West Cork. She visited Bill's extraordinary operation many times to buy his cheese, and sometimes on a hot summer's day they would share a glass of wine in the cooling shed beneath the soothing whirr of the refrigeration fan.

Bill Hogan's converted farmhouse lies about two miles outside Schull, on the east side and inland. Characteristically for the region, the approach to the buildings is along a small and winding boreen over a rough and uneven surface and leads straight into the yard. On the immediate right is a converted shed, and in front stands the converted farmhouse. Both are now almost entirely turned over to the business of cheesemaking.

Bill leads me and photographer John Minihan into a back room that contains the implements of his business: an elaborate and old-fashioned boiler and a large stainless-steel sink. An unusual aroma pervades the room – the smell of the product in the preparation stages is not as pleasant as the end result! The cheesemaker, a slight man in his sixties, leads us up the stairs to his living quarters.

We sit at an old wooden table and Bill places a large wedge of cheese in front of us. 'It is too early for it now,' suggests our host, 'perhaps later with a glass of wine.' That sounds good to us. Bill has a light, precise voice and while he is clearly an enthusiastic conversationalist, he chooses his words carefully when talking of the murder. It is as if the terrible tragedy has induced an unnatural caution among the people of Schull and its surrounds. This caution is something that I have noticed again and again since my arrival, but then I am a stranger and I have not hidden the purpose of my visit, so it is no surprise that suspicion should be the first reaction. I am hopeful that it will soon be replaced by acceptance. This, thankfully, proves to be the case, because in the end everyone wants a resolution. The murder has caused too much damage for silence.

Our conversation starts with the murder, its effect on the community and theories about the possible motive for the killing and the identity of the killer. I am anxious to get a local's reaction to these theories, particularly the one that falsely portrayed Daniel Toscan du Plantier as a disaffected husband who had taken a contract out on his wife with a professional hitman. We agree that the story about Daniel is ridiculous and that whoever propagated it had not thought it out logically or rationally. Bill did not go along with this, nor with any of the other theories, and he believes, as do most people in the area, that the killer lives in West Cork.

Bill talks of the terror, fear and loathing that seeped through every part of the community in the wake of the killing. It was felt acutely by those, like Bill, who had encountered Sophie during her visits over the years.

'The effect was all the greater, as nothing remotely like this had ever happened in the area before, and because of the fact that Sophie was such a beautiful, gentle woman who was liked and respected by everyone who had met her. It was just horrible to think that the killer may be living in the region. An added dimension was that it was Christmastime, which in a close-knit community means a time for generosity and love, a time for family and good spirit.

'It was awful that first Christmas. We were supposed to have a big party in the factory downstairs. I was going to cancel it but the Gardaí said to go ahead and try to have a Christmas. But it wasn't the same. As the weeks went by, the feeling of emptiness, loss and fear just got worse and worse. And, you know, it never goes away. Since then, Christmas is always a reminder of this tragedy. Everyone wants the killer brought to trial.'

In such cases in Ireland, it is ultimately a matter for the Director of Public Prosecutions to assess the evidence presented and to decide whether or not to proceed with a prosecution and trial. To date, there has been no decision to prosecute in the Du Plantier murder.

Bill first met Sophie in 1993 through Leo Bolger, who she had employed to do most of the renovations to her farmhouse in Dunmanus West.

'At that time Leo lived fairly close to Sophie in what could be described as a gingerbread house and he carried out all, or nearly all of the renovation work. Leo gave Sophie some of my cheese and she said that she really loved it. One day she called me on the phone. "This is Sophie Bouniol," she said, and asked if it would be all right to come over to buy some of the cheese. Of course I was delighted that a Frenchwoman had found the cheese so tasty.

'The first time she came over she made an immediate impression with me, as she did with many others. She was striking looking, very elegantly dressed and with a sweet, quavering voice. She seemed to me an urban refugee and she clearly loved this part of West Cork. Although quiet-spoken, she was very direct and could look you straight in the eye, the way a self-assured and independent woman would.'

Bill recalls Sophie calling over many times after that, nearly always accompanied by someone – her son, or other women whom he took to be friends or relatives. On two occasions she was alone.

'The first was a scorching hot summer's day. I had some lovely Luxembourg wine, so we went in to the building where I mature the cheese and we had a glass of wine and ate some cheese. We stood right under the cooling fan, which was very pleasant. She was not a woman for small talk, but I think we were on the same wavelength. I am a member of Amnesty International, and Sophie was concerned with human rights. She might have been a woman with money, but she had all the right values. She was passionate about what she did and she cared about people.'

Bill is not just a cheesemaker, he is also a poet and as such is a keen observer of people. He was impressed both with Sophie's beauty and her sense of style. She reminded him of Catherine Deneuve, an actress whose serene beauty is the epitome of elegance and who is as beautiful now as ever, seemingly impervious to the passage of time.

During one visit, Sophie told Bill that she intended to spend more time in West Cork. Bill asked her what her life in Paris was like. She paused and replied, 'In Paris, my life is like a multi-storey.'

That ended the conversation. Afterwards, and particularly since the murder, the cheesemaker has often wondered about the meaning of this rather enigmatic statement. We discussed it and came to the conclusion that Sophie meant her life was complicated and multi-layered.

'Yes, that is an impression that I got of Sophie,' Bill agrees. 'She was so charming and mannerly, but sometimes she would just cut the conversation dead. I would say that there was always something going on inside her head. She was deep, and sometimes that depth can bring a sort of sadness, which, on several occasions, I saw in her eyes.'

Sophie called to Bill for the last time during August or September of 1996. 'I remember it so clearly because she looked stunning. She was wearing a dress of silk material, which could have come straight out of a fashion magazine; something you expect to see in the middle of Paris. She had this very fine make-up and a magnificent piece of jewellery around her neck. I invited her to have a glass of wine, but she apologised and said that she was in a hurry and on the way to a meeting in Paris.'

Sophie ordered a whole Desmond cheese, which cost over IR£60, and explained that she was giving the cheese as a present to a person attending the meeting. Smiling, she added that she was going to keep half for herself. 'She drove off and I never saw her again,' Bill says, with a sigh that expresses emptiness and a hint of despair. We return to our discussion on the effect of the continuing presence of the killer.

'We cannot believe that the Garda investigation has not yet reaped the reward it deserves,' says Bill. 'Right from the beginning, the detectives have behaved with great courtesy and respect to members of the community and got the full co-operation and backing of the people. I know scores of people who have given statements and I am one of them. If the police say, as they do in many murder cases, that public co-operation is vital, they could rarely have got the level of co-operation that they received from the people of Schull and the area.

'We are bitterly disappointed that, first of all, Sophie's death has not been resolved, and that the murderer is still free. There will be no peace in this countryside until justice is done and the killer punished.'

It is a view universally shared by the people in this area of West Cork, anxious to banish the poisonous atmosphere and remove the stain that has blackened the landscape. There is nothing but frustration with the delay in justice being served.

During our conversation, an English couple and Bill's business partner and his son drop in. One gets a sense of the nature of the neighbourhood: open doors and trust. The sort of trust that Sophie would have noticed and which would undoubtedly have given her a feeling of safety, though she herself maintained a more reserved approach.

In fact, Sophie had told her parents and brother that one of the things she loved most about the area was the local custom of leaving the key in the door and the invitation to help herself to whatever she was short of: tea, sugar, milk, anything. Since her murder, locks and security devices have taken on an unprecedented importance in Schull and its environs.

Bill leads us back down the wooden steps and into the yard. He invites us into the curing shed and we stand under the cooling fan where Sophie drank her glass of Luxembourg wine. We eat a slice or two of the organic cheese that is stacked on wooden shelves and I understand how she would have marvelled at the sheer simplicity and efficiency of this operation – the very definition of a cottage industry, and all the more attractive for that.

We have walked a while in Sophie's shadow and have found it comforting. We have been given a sense of the living woman and of the qualities that defined her easy interaction with the people of the area. It re-confirms how much she was valued, and the standing in which she was held.

Some time after this conversation I spoke to Leo Bolger. Leo endorses all of Bill's impressions of their French neighbour. 'She was a lovely and courteous woman and very popular with everyone who came into contact with her. Sophie was very friendly, and above all, genuine. I first met her shortly after she bought the house. I lived about half a mile away and she asked me to do some work on the house, which I did for the next number of years. She changed very little in the interior from the time she moved in. It seemed to me that Sophie liked and wanted to preserve the original feel of the building.

'I did very basic things: repair work, maintenance, work on the roof if there were missing slates, something which was quite common with the high winds in this part of the country. The only concession to modernisation was the installation of central heating. This was absolutely necessary because it is very cold in the winter.'

Leo and his wife Sally, who now run a horse-riding school in Dunbeacon, have found the shock of Sophie's murder hard to get over, not just because of the ghastly manner of her death, but also because her killer is still on the loose.

'It was so shocking,' says Leo. 'It is still almost unbeliev-able to this day. This place, or the people, will never be the same again. Everyone wants the killer brought to justice.'

Later I visit poet John Montague and his partner, the novelist Elizabeth Wassell, who collaborated on an article about the murder for the The *New Yorker*. Elizabeth has also written a novel that was partly inspired by the event, *The Thing He Loves*, which she wrote in an effort to deal with the aftermath and implications of the killing.

In the novel, a woman is murdered. Her killer is arrested, tried and imprisoned. In prison he loses none of the sense of his own importance, continually reinforcing it by avidly reading every account of the murder and the trial that he can lay his hands on. Of the real murder in West Cork, Elizabeth remarks to me that the locals do not savour the tragedy or the notoriety it brought to their townland. In her book she described the feeling: 'All summer lightness van-ished. No one exclaimed any more about the splendid weather. Music no longer flowed from the pubs. People moved around the road with heavy faces.'

Over a glass of wine, we discuss the murder that inspired Elizabeth's novel and the hundreds of thousands of news-paper words. John Montague, a distinguished-looking man with twinkling blue eyes and a ruddy, youthful complexion, sits beside Elizabeth, a small, dark-haired woman with large, intense brown eyes. Sun spills into the kitchen – like many kitchens in this part of the world it is small but welcoming, a legacy of times when the kitchen was the most used room in the house.

'I had spent the days before that Christmas with Elizabeth at the Literary Forum in Okinawa,' says John. 'Okinawa is an elongated, serrated island that regards its larger neighbour [Japan] with much the same ambivalence as Ireland does England. We had gone there from Tokyo, where I had been granted an audience with the Empress. On the flight home I learned about the murder and realised we were heading back into turbulence.'

After their *New Yorker* article was published in January 2000, there were threatening calls left on the answer phone telling John that he was not wanted in the area and that he should leave. Montague makes light of the calls now, but he was sufficiently worried at the time to be relieved to resume his regular trips abroad. His house, despite its pleasing location, is isolated, like many in the area, and is therefore vulnerable to attack. The fear and loathing that followed in the wake of the murder seem a long distance away now, on this bright summer's evening, but those feelings have not diminished. John describes the atmosphere as a poisonous feeling combined with a sense of disgrace for the crime committed against the popular Frenchwoman and her family. In his *New Yorker* article he wrote about the lack of resolution in the case and the effect this had:

'Perhaps there will be no real conclusion, and the cloud that settled over West Cork in the aftermath of the murder will gradually dissipate, leaving only the faint impression of fear and foreboding it brought to a place that had not been similarly sullied for decades. Yet there is something too distilled and concentrated about this story for it to disappear quickly. It seems to be part of a particularly European drama – for which West Cork is only one of many stages.'

The poet articulates the dilemma perfectly: on the one hand people would like the terrible memory of those dark days of December 1996 and January 1997 to fade into oblivion, but on the other hand, until the soul of Sophie is appeased and justice done for her family, there can be no peace of mind for the people of West Cork because they are forced to keep remembering, forced to keep that dreadful event alive.

There is, Daniel Toscan du Plantier has said, 'a devil somewhere in the hills of southern Ireland'. Acts such as these create undeniable tensions in the area and community in which they take place, all the more so where the occurrence is such a rarity. There is a legacy of both sadness and horror to be dealt with and the unspoken is far more potent because it recognises the unutterable evil of the murder. The unspoken condemnation within the silence is indeed deafening.

Part Two

A WOMAN OF SUBSTANCE

Chapter Five

SOPHIE – THE PERSON
Meeting the Bouniol Family in West Cork

While in Schull, I hear that Sophie's parents, Georges and Marguerite Bouniol, and her aunt, Marie Madeleine Opalka, are on holiday in the area and staying in Sophie's house. They have not spoken to the media in the past six years because of the upsetting and often untruthful things that were written about Sophie at the time of the murder, when the media frenzy was at its height. These reports were carried in both Irish and French newspapers, thus spreading rumours, mixed in with some of the facts, in her native country as well as throughout Ireland.

The family got together and made a collective decision never to speak to the media on the subject of Sophie's death, or their feelings about it. Although it was rumoured to the contrary, I have also learned that they never shared the criticism of the Garda investigation and, over the past six years, have had a very good relationship with at least one of the leading investigators who kept them up-to-date with any developments in the case.

Each December since the murder, Marguerite, Georges and Marie Madeleine, as well as other members of Sophie's family, have returned to West Cork for a memorial Mass for Sophie in Goleen church. This is clearly an act of courage, as it cannot be easy to return to the place where Sophie was so brutally taken from them. It must also be some consolation to the people of the area to know that Sophie's family have not rejected the country and the location she loved so dearly.

Through a source, I make contact with the family and speak to Marie Madeleine Opalka, Sophie's aunt, sister of her mother.

She proposes that we meet at the Bantry Bay Hotel in Bantry two days later at 2.30pm. Sophie's father and mother will be present and they will decide after that meeting whether or not to co-operate. They would prefer to meet in a private room. I ring the owner, Vivian O'Callaghan, and he kindly provides an upstairs room out of the public gaze.

The day of our appointment is a beautiful summer's day. As the car comes down the hill from the Westlodge Hotel just outside of town, we pass by the Abbey cemetery, which contains a monument to the men, both Irish and French, who perished when the *Betelgeuse* oil-tanker exploded at Whiddy Island in 1979. Rounding the bend, the full panorama of Bantry Bay is revealed.

We pass by Bantry House, which also has a connection to France. The mansion of the earls of Bantry was packed full of magnificent French furniture. The second earl was an avid collector and, just by luck, he happened to be in Paris after the revolution when the contents of the royal houses were being put up for auction. Included in the collection he brought back to Bantry were tapestries ordered by Louis XV for Marie Antoinette on the occasion of her marriage to the Dauphin, as well as a Napoleonic fireplace, tables and writing desks.

From the town square, a statue of Brendan the Navigator gazes out over the harbour wall. The sun sparkles on the surface of the sea, the haze above the harbour giving the scene a slight sense of the surreal. But in the upstairs room of the hotel it is if this scene never existed.

There, for the first time, I meet Sophie's parents and her aunt. Marie Madeleine is a formidable and highly intelligent woman, married to Roman Opalka, a Polish artist of note. Marie Madeleine cuts a striking figure, dressed in black and sporting a stylish, broad-brimmed black hat. Georges Bouniol is a small, handsome, dapper man with a fine head of silver hair, and his wife, Marguerite, is slim, petite and elegantly dressed. The resemblance to Sophie is immediately recognisable in her eyes.

The Bouniols do not speak much English, so Marie

Madeleine translates everything. Over a three-hour period we discuss the history of the tragedy that has so cruelly beset the family, which, like many families from the south-central region of France, is incredibly close.

They are all naturally disappointed that after the passage of six years the investigation has not achieved a result, but they are full of praise for the leading members of the investigation team who have kept in touch and have been incredibly sympathetic. They realise how frustrating it is for the police to have forwarded two files to the office of the Director of Public Prosecutions, and not to be given the green light to proceed with a prosecution.

We begin to talk about the crime and I mention that the murder of Sophie achieved a very high profile because of her beauty, background and connections – the case would have reverberations on an international scale, far beyond the scene of the crime in West Cork.

But we focus on the close-knit nature of a rural community that has been riven by paranoia and suspicion by the brutality of the crime and by the fact that the killer is still free and may be living in the region. In the early stages of a murder investigation there is often a collective suspicion as well as a sense of collective guilt – this dreadful thing has happened in *their* place. Layers of privacy that have been jealously guarded are peeled back and secrets that have no direct bearing on the case, but whose owners would prefer them not to see the light of day, can be revealed. And once the more faint-hearted have retreated into their shells, it can take years for those shells to open or be prised open. Everyone suffers as a result.

Even as we are speaking, in June 2002, I am aware that an enquiry into the processes and effectiveness of the investigation into the Du Plantier murder has just been completed. Senior detectives from Dublin have reviewed every aspect of the case, re-interviewed witnesses and examined the procedures of the Gardaí involved in the original investigation. These detectives have presented a new report to the Director of Public Prosecutions's office. It is believed that the enquiry has uncovered nothing new, but has also not found anything wrong with the first investigation. The new report points out the thoroughness of the investigation and the necessity of bringing the case to trial and to a conclusion.

We discuss the irony of the fact that Sophie loved Ireland so much and yet it was in her adopted country that fate dealt her this terrible hand. Her family appreciate this, but are still committed to the country and to West Cork, simply because of Sophie's love for the place. It was Sophie's choice to have this house as her retreat from her hectic life in France and a place where she could bring family and friends. Her family honour her decision. They are at pains to emphasise to me that while Sophie used the house as a retreat, it was never to escape anything that was going on in her life. When things went wrong she faced up to the ensuing problems. They say that she always came to Dunmanus West with a purpose, whether that was to rest, or to work.

This week, for the first time since the death, they are staying at the house in Toormore. It is very painful to have to pass the site of the murder on a daily basis, but the family are prepared to endure this hurt in order that the memory of Sophie be kept alive. They hope against hope that their ongoing visits will be a reminder of the tragedy, and may eventually inspire someone who has yet to come forward to help bring about the justice they long for. It is probably futile to think that their presence pricks the conscience of the perpetrator himself.

We finish our conversation and I am delighted when Georges and Marguerite Bouniol and Marie Madeleine Opalka agree to co-operate in putting together this book. I assure them that it will treat their daughter and niece with something other than the tag of victim, a label that suits the killer down to the ground because it depersonalises the woman he has brutalised and makes little of her terrible death. It feeds into the way he thinks about women, as objects to be used for his satisfaction. Instead, I tell them, my hope is to come to know Sophie, the person.

We agree to meet the following day in Sophie's house. Although I had been to the site once before while researching an article for the *Sunday Independent*, I had not been beyond the main gate. While much has been written about the location, and numerous pictures taken of the exterior of the house, I felt that going inside, especially in the company of Sophie's family, would provide invaluable new insights and give me a chance to get in touch with the real woman whose imprint would surely be all over the house she made her own.

* * *

When I open the gate at the bottom of the laneway I am confronted by the memorial to Sophie on the right-hand side. Some years before, the family had erected this low-sized Celtic cross at the spot where the body was found. A bunch of faded flowers lies on the plinth, mostly wild flowers, like goldenrod and the ubiquitous fuchsia that has become an emblem for West Cork. Some letters are half-hidden by the leaves; I pull them aside and reveal the one-word inscription: *Sophie*. Behind the cross there is a low, mossy drystone wall topped by a few strands of barbed wire and almost overgrown by ferns, briars and nettles.

The white house is perched two hundred feet above sea level, on an elevation looking out over sloping fields and rocky ridges that stretch down to Toormore Bay and the wider expanse of Roaring Water Bay. It is a bigger house than I expected, with five upstairs windows set in at roof level and an extended front porch. A converted farmhouse, it sits naturally into its rural surroundings in a way that many of the purpose-built holiday homes dotted around West Cork do not.

The uphill laneway swings around in a loop to the right before curving back left towards the house and on behind it to the house of Shirley Foster and Alfie Lyons. I walk up the laneway and at the top of the hill turn towards the porch. Madame Opalka opens the door and leads me in to the living-room. Before leaving Schull I had bought a bouquet of flowers for Sophie's mother, Marguerite. I hand them to her and am not surprised when she says that they will be for Sophie.

We sit around a table, drinking tea and talking about the fateful Christmas of 1996. Madame Opalka describes herself as very close to her niece – a godmother to whom Sophie could look in times of stress or trouble in her life. She recalls how Sophie had told her she was coming to Toormore for a short break.

'Sophie was really exhausted, as she had just finished a documentary for the Arte channel. She asked at least five people to come to Ireland with her, but at Christmas everyone had plans. It might have been different at another time. She rang me up and said, "Please come with me, Marie Madeleine, please," but I could not contemplate leaving my husband over the holiday. She repeated that she was so exhausted and really needed someone to go to Ireland with her.

'She asked her mother, but Marguerite had just come back from visiting her youngest son, Stephane, in New York and was too tired to face another journey. She asked her best friend Agnes Thomas, but she could not come, and Daniel could not go either. It seems so terrible now. Oh why, oh why did I not go? This terrible tragedy would not have happened if I had gone with Sophie.'

Madame Opalka breaks down in tears at the memory and at the cruel twist of fate that might have been changed … if only. Georges and Marguerite have also become tearful, tortured by the possibility that if even one other person had been there the killer would have been discouraged from pursuing his opportunity. It seems to them now that they were not there for Sophie in her hour of need. Of course that is not true, but this is obviously a very real guilt that they still feel as strongly as they did six years ago.

It is heartbreaking to see the Bouniols and Marie Madeleine turn their pain and anger back on themselves. Their beloved Sophie had been left alone – not that anyone at the time felt that she was in any danger. Hindsight is cruel rather than comforting in such circumstances. Marguerite and Georges are no different from any other parents – they would willingly sacrifice their own lives for those of their children. It is unnatural for children to die before their parents.

And Sophie was taken in her prime. A beautiful, highly intelligent woman who loved literature and poetry and had so much to contribute.

In the aftermath of the murder the family re-ran every conversation, examining every nuance for clues or signs of what was to come. In this way the chronicle of Sophie's last days can be innocently transformed to one of a death foretold. It is a hurtful process, as the family trawl the minutes and hours for signs that they did not see or appreciate. Marie Madeleine wonders whether her niece had a premonition of some sort. Marguerite agrees. She felt that there was something amiss after Sophie had called her on the phone just before she left for Cork.

Her last words to her mother were '*Adieu, Maman*', instead of the more common '*Au revoir*'. The sense of finality in this unusual farewell from Sophie made her mother feel uncomfortable. Marguerite wanted to call Sophie back, but did not.

They tell me that two months earlier, when Sophie and her husband Daniel arrived at their country home in Ambax, Sophie stopped a woodcutter from trimming trees in the cemetery where she would be laid to rest. On another occasion, she compared the palm of her hand with those of her aunt and mother, and commented that her lifeline was only half as long as theirs. She was dreading the thought of reaching the age of forty; she felt her years falling away quickly.

Marguerite also remembers how Sophie was fond of a

ring that Marguerite wore and had asked her for it. 'I had the ring, but did not give it at the time. I said that I would give it to Sophie at Christmas.' She never got the opportunity, and to this moment she regrets it deeply because she reads something like foreboding into her daughter's request.

The Bouniols are not the type of people who have luck to thank for the previous good fortune of their lives. They are serious and dedicated people who have worked hard for everything they have achieved. And, until December 1996, they also had no reason to rail against any misfortune. Even now, they show no signs of rage. I ask Marguerite if she was inclined to curse the heavens. 'No', she says quietly. 'I just do not believe in anything anymore.'

It is quite a devastating statement from a woman and mother who has lived her life to a strict moral Roman Catholic code. She has been reduced to questioning a tradition that had been in her family for generations. Photos I see later of the family are peppered with prominent religious occasions: First Holy Communions, baptisms, church weddings. And now all that effort, all that belief, for nothing. The devil who preyed on their daughter in Toormore has had an impact even he could not have imagined.

We return to the inevitable sifting through the last acts that stand out before Sophie left Paris and to the foreboding and premonition her family now feel they sensed in her at the time. Sophie was normally such an independent, fearless creature that it was out of character for her to appeal to so many people to accompany her on the trip.

Marie Madeleine says that Sophie rang her from the airport on 20 December before she left for Ireland. 'She was so close to me, closer than my own two daughters. She was always so affectionate and kind. I remember when Pascale, her brother Bertrand's wife, had had a new baby boy. After visiting the maternity hospital, Sophie called me and was worried about the baby. She said no one is giving him enough milk. She then said that she would like to have a child with Daniel. She also told Pascale that she would like another child.'

When Sophie was looking for a house in Ireland, it was Alexandra, Marie Madeleine's daughter, who accompanied her on the tour of West Cork and Kerry.

Sophie narrowed the choice down to two: the farmhouse in Dunmanus West and one on the seashore. According to her mother, Alexandra preferred the house by the sea; the farmhouse gave her an ominous feeling. The location was too isolated for her liking and she felt what she described to her mother as 'something very strange'. The elevation of the house exposes it to the elements, particularly the wind, which kept Alexandra awake the whole of one night she spent alone in the cottage. She told Marie Madeleine that she was terrified and would never spend another night there on her own. But the sense of isolation appealed to Sophie. She had not chosen the house as a conventional 'summer house', but as a retreat where she could work and think in peace.

* * *

While Sophie's parents and aunt and the photographer, John Minihan, converse, I ask if I may roam around the house to get the feel of it and to get a sense of Sophie and her tastes. I leave them downstairs and go upstairs and into Sophie's bedroom.

Monastic would be the way to describe the room. It is small and cell-like. There is an old wooden desk in the middle of it, facing the window and the distant sea view. On this Sophie kept her notepaper and pens, and she sat on an old wooden chair while she wrote. The bed is elevated so that she could get the full effect of the view and especially the Fastnet lighthouse in the distance.

The lighthouse, which is built on Fastnet Rock, clearly held a fascination for Sophie. Its flashing light illuminated her room at night. There is a model of the lighthouse on a wooden shelf beside her bed, a framed photograph of it on the wall, and in the upstairs corridor further photographs of it, one a dramatic aerial shot with the sea pounding the lighthouse. There is little doubt that she had acquainted herself with its history.

The Fastnet stands four-and-a-half miles out into the Alantic, equidistant from the west end of Cape Clear and from Crookhaven, where Sophie used to visit O'Sullivan's bar and restaurant. The Fastnet is actually two rocks, the larger towering 147 feet above the sea, and divided from the other rock, the Little Fastnet, by a narrow indentation in the rock face. The rocks are known in folk and nautical history as 'Paddy's Milestone' and 'Teardrop of Ireland' because, as the crowded emigrant ships steamed towards America, it was the last sight the departing passengers saw of their native land. Some would never see Ireland again.

With its distinctive shape and the magnificent but hazardous setting, the rock and the lighthouse seem to be making a solitary stand against danger.

Sir Robert Ball, the scientific adviser to the Commissioner of Irish Lights, visited the lighthouse shortly after its completion and wrote: 'As to the beams of the Fastnet, during all the time of our return to harbour I can only describe them as magnificent. At ten miles distant, the great revolving spokes of light, succeeding each other at intervals of five seconds, gave the most distinctive character possible … each flash as it swept past lighted up the ship and the rigging like a searchlight.'

This was the flash, from the now unmanned lighthouse, that Sophie found so fascinating. In the silent hours of a winter night it would act almost as watchful eye, regularly lighting up the enveloping darkness.

I notice that a piece of white material bordered by a fringe has been draped across the window. This strikes me as odd, as it would hamper the view that Sophie was so fond of. When I ask Marguerite about it later she says that this is her shawl. Unike her daughter, she is not keen on the Fastnet light and finds the flashes disturbing and ominous.

To the left of Sophie's bed is a wooden shelf containing her book collection for bedtime reading. Everything is stark and so simply laid out – as if Sophie needed to be alone with her muse and did not want any distraction. Comfortable but sparse is how I would describe it.

This atmosphere strikes me as being very much in keeping with the spirit of the original farmhouse. I am very moved by this; I expected a more lavish interior. I expected, even, a 'French feeling' to the house. But no, Sophie had attuned herself to the Irish origins of the house rather than forcing it to conform to a French style. When visiting friends or shopping in Schull, Sophie was the epitome of French style, good taste and sophistication. But her Irish home was utterly true to its original simple design. Josephine Hellen had already told me that television was banned in the house in Toormore, although Sophie did bring a stereo with her so that she could listen to music while she wrote.

A brief glance at the book titles confirms her broad taste

in reading. A Virginia Woolf novel stands alongside a collection by her favourite poet, WB Yeats. Canadian author Paul Auster sits next to a collection of stories by William Trevor. Next comes JM Synge, Thomas de Quincey and Theophile Gautier. On the living-room shelf downstairs I had noticed more poetry collections and two old Agatha Christie murder mysteries, one with a covered corpse on the cover.

Everything in the house is minimal and mostly painted in white. There is no ostentation, no pretentiousness. The narrow upstairs corridor has Sophie's bedroom, a bathroom, then a second bedroom with bunk beds and finally the third and largest bedroom, where Sophie was sleeping on the night the killer came to the house. This is the warmest room in the house, large and spacious and with a bathroom off to the gable end. The few pieces of furniture are old, and the bed is just a mattress on the floor. And yet the predominant feeling is of a neat and tidy space.

I am overwhelmed by a sense of Sophie's presence. Below I hear the muted conversation of her mother and father, and then the sonorous voice of Marie Madeleine engaging with the ringing tones of the photographer. The contrast between this jovial normality and the absent presence of Sophie makes me feel warm and chilled at the same time. It is hard not to think of the last night that Sophie slept in this bed, in this room, peaceful and unsuspecting, and then to let one's thoughts go to the dreadful events that followed.

My mind returns again to Yeats's poem, which Sophie was reading before she fell asleep on her final night. The extraordinary coincidence of this is eerie, not only because of its subject matter but also because this is a poem with a French connection – it was written in December 1891 for Yeats's great love Maud Gonne, who was recovering from exhaustion in the south of France. It has disturbing resonances now, in the wake of Sophie's murder.

A Dream of Death
WB Yeats
I dreamed that one had died in a strange place
Near no accustomed hand;
And they had nailed the boards above her face,
The peasants of that land,
Wondering to lay her in that solitude,
And raised above her mound
A cross they had made out of two bits of wood,
And planted cypress round;
And left her to the indifferent stars above
Until I carved these words:
She was more beautiful than thy first love,
But now lies under boards.

I look out the window at the slate- and green-coloured rocky hill that obscures the view of the house from Kilfeadda bridge. For a moment it does not seem so bleak anymore; there is even a parting in the overhanging cloud. But, as my gaze descends from the hill and the sky to the stony, barbed-wire fenced field below, the sly, loping form of a fox suddenly slinks across the grass and surreptitiously slides under the cover of the hedgerow. A shiver ascends my spine and I know that the bed is really empty and Sophie's presence is truly an absence.

An eleven-step wooden stairway leads to the sitting room downstairs. The end of the stairway faces the side wall of the house, which contains a fireplace. At the other end of the room, in the opposite wall, there is another fireplace, huge by today's standards, forming a niche in the wall tall enough for someone to stand in, and with stone seats on either side. This would have been the traditional farmhouse fireplace, where the cooking would have been done in pots hanging from an iron crook over the fire. Pokers and a bellows stand beside the grate, and I notice that an old horseshoe, a symbol of good luck, has been nailed to the back wall of the fireplace.

The room is decorated with pictures of seascapes and traditional hunting scenes, red-coated men in tall hats galloping over the countryside. There are white candles everywhere – in sconces on the wall, in the fireplace niches and on the mantelpiece.

Halfway down on the side wall is a door into the front porch. At the right-hand side of the bottom wall is a small passageway that leads into the little kitchen. This room is the closest to what the original farmhouse would have been like. There is a rough-hewn wooden table beside the window to the front, where Sophie sat reading on the fateful night, her feet propped up on the chair opposite her. The kitchen is tiny, almost claustrophobic, and while it is not cluttered, there is hardly room to move about. Even to the uninitiated eye, it is not difficult to take in the entire contents of the space almost at once. Sophie would sit between the table and the window, near the radiator, where there would be warmth on a cold winter's night.

Across from the table, directly under the other kitchen window, there is another small wooden table next to an old-style porcelain sink perched on a concrete-brick base. This is how it must have been too in the previous life of the farmhouse. Here is the strongest testament that Sophie liked to keep the simple things simple, and maintained the soul of the house's former existence intact. The place could be a hundred years old. It has a warm, homely feel to it. Sophie's sense of honouring the past and the tradition of former inhabitants is everywhere in this house.

An old-style wooden door with a latch leads out of the kitchen into a small room that doubles as a pantry and a utility room, containing a fridge and washing machine and shelves of foodstuffs. The rear door leads out onto a small, roughly-paved stone patio. This side of the house is the least attractive. Once off the stone patio there is rough ground and rock constantly jutting out of the grass. Leaving aside the benefit of hindsight, there is not a good feeling or atmosphere here, and at night, because of its sheltered aspect, it would be as dark as a dungeon and a perfect stomping ground and hiding place for a predator. Such a predator would have the advantage of surprise when the rear door was opened. One foot in the door would prevent closure and outside there is nowhere to run and nowhere to hide.

The immediate surroundings of Sophie's house are rugged and untamed. And this was where Sophie, trapped by the intruder, searched desperately for an escape route. I follow in her footsteps. Opposite the door is an old shed with a sagging, galvanised iron roof. It is surrounded by wild overgrowth with a profusion of nettles and briars. It is, to all intents and purposes, a trap – no matter where you turn there are only obstacles. To the right of the small stone patio a large iron gate prevents access to a laneway.

Looking in the opposite direction, to the left, you encounter bushy briars and high, overgrown grass. The entrance to a field is cut off by a barbed-wire fence, with just a very small space between the wooden stake that marks the end of the fence and a wall in front of the house. It is possible to squeeze through this aperture, but it would hamper a person in flight considerably.

This tiny space provides access to a field that inclines to such a degree that it is difficult to stay upright while walking. Ascending the field is made treacherous by rocks which jut up through the uneven surface and at running pace would cause one to lose balance. Descending it at night, as Sophie did, would be even more difficult.

The decision to go to the rear door, and use that side of the house which provides all the obstacles to escape, as opposed to the front entrance, was a smart move from the killer's point of view. The front entrance would be a more risky option in terms of identification. If he had approached the front porch, he would have been clearly visibly to Sophie under the porch light and she would certainly not have opened the door had she caught sight of him. The darkness and roughness at the back of the house suited his mission.

There is a severe drop through rough terrain from the space between the fence and the wall to the point where Sophie's body was found. At the bottom, where three laneways converge, are hedges, a barbed-wire fence, thorns and rocks. The fencing is low but impossible to clear, especially at night.

Just at the exit to the laneway from the field, there is a

concrete gatepost on top of which lie a number of large cavity blocks, identical to the second murder weapon. Even in a storm of rage and adrenalin, only a strong man could lift one of those blocks. I attempted to raise one and could not get it above my waist. I can hardly contemplate the damage such a block could inflict on a human skull and the utter lack of necessity of using it when the killer did.

The selection of such a weapon and the strength needed to utilise it, as well as the psychological make-up required for such a brutal act, provide valuable clues to the personality and profile of the killer. How many people could achieve this act?

The fresh bouquet lies alongside the faded flowers on Sophie's memorial. I look out beyond the gate towards the rocky ridge and the boreen, turning and twisting into the distance. Even if Sophie had made it out beyond the gate, she could never have negotiated this terrain on foot. It would be hard to keep one's bearing here, even in a car. Just the day before, a local taxi driver, with a very good knowledge of the area, took the wrong turning, leading us way off the path, and only got it right the second time round. The killer held all the ace cards. It might have taken him time, but he would have still hunted her down.

I return to the house up the laneway, following the steps that the killer must have taken. At the low, traditional drystone wall that surrounds the front of the house, I look out across the valley. Somewhere in West Cork is the man responsible for the grief I have witnessed inside in the house and for the unease that permeates the whole of this beautiful land.

Chapter Six

SOPHIE – AT HOME
Rendezvous in Paris

Georges and Marguerite greet me warmly and show me around their magnificent apartment, with its large, spacious rooms and fabulous high ceilings. It is impeccably furnished, and everything is in its place: evidence of the couple's ordered and tidy nature. Yet the visitor, though impressed, is not overwhelmed, because pomposity never gets in the way of style. In the huge, airy and light-filled living-room there is a large display of family photographs, all framed.

I applaud the apartment's style and taste, and the diminutive Mme Bouniol protests, '*Non, non.*' But I know that she and her husband are justifiably proud, because it is a lifetime's reward for work and contains a lifetime's memories of both family and careers. And to them it is the history clearly visible inside this apartment that is important.

The photographs are those that in the normal course of events remain within slightly dusty album covers, to be quickly cleaned off and opened on special occasions, the pages turned with pride, disbelief at the passage of time and constant amusement. But things are different now for this family. There is the need never to forget and to have visual aids to bring back the memories of better, happier times.

Sophie's brother, Bertrand, counselled his mother that, while he understood her need to create a shrine for her daughter, other members of the family should be included. It was sensible and excellent advice. Apart from the few individual portraits, stunning and revealing as they are, the photographs now on display provide a touching record of the progress of an individual through various stages of her life accompanied by the family that mattered to her – her mother, father, brothers, cousins, her favourite aunt Marie Madeleine, her son Pierre Louis.

There is a photograph, tinted red by the summer evening sun, of Marguerite as a young woman, on holiday in Spain with her two eldest children. They are sitting on a promenade wall with the blue sea stretching towards a headland in the background. Five-year-old Sophie has a distinctly cheeky, boyish expression, while three-year-old Bertrand wears a beatific smile. Marguerite, dressed in white trousers and a patterned short-sleeved top, looks at the camera, her serious and determined nature showing in her eyes. The sun is behind Georges as he snaps the camera shutter and his shadow appears on the lower part of the wall and on Marguerite's legs.

It is a golden time and looking at that portrait of the innocent pleasure of childhood, I realise that the moment is frozen in time but its impact has changed utterly. What should be joyous nostalgia has been cruelly transformed into painful contemplation of what was and also of what should have been. Looking at it, you cannot help bringing with you the haunting knowledge of what was to be, the cruel fate that stamped itself on this happy, lovely, loved and loving little girl.

We all look at the picture and in a double exposure I catch sight of the parents in the mirror. I cannot keep my eyes from that cheeky little face and can only imagine the pain it now conjures up for the family. Georges and Marguerite are good people. Their pride in this history that they have created is just one of the things that has been so unfairly stolen from them. It brings home to me that the family of a murder victim suffer not just the trauma of the immediate loss of their loved one but are also robbed of the hopes and expectations they had for the future of that person.

There is a picture of Sophie's First Communion, taken outside the main door of Notre Dame Cathedral in Paris. Marie Madeleine, glamorous as a film star, adjusts the cap-like veil on the head of her adored niece. Sophie herself looks like a beautiful little Nordic princess, wearing a long white habit with a crucifix around her neck. She glances away from the camera, smiling on the occasion of her special day. Marie Madeleine's daughters, Sophie's first cousins Alexandra and Patricia, are at either side, with Bertrand lurking in the shadow behind Patricia, like a little artful dodger.

I try to imagine what it would be like to look at this if the young girl had been your own flesh and blood. People close to the investigation, who have dealt with the Bouniols over the years, have witnessed grief but never anger. This too is my experience of them, short as it has been.

I put myself in their position and find no restraint, only the hot sword of revenge burning in my heart. I recall someone saying to me that if anyone harmed her children she 'would swing for' the perpetrator, meaning she would be willing to be hanged for revenge. I am afraid I would fall into that uncivilised category.

The pain will never end for the Bouniols. I have seen it in the house in Dunmanus West and now again, heartbreakingly, at her childhood home in Paris. Her parents show me into what was Sophie's narrow, high-ceilinged room. It has been much transformed because it was taken over by her youngest brother, Stephane, after she had left the house. But there is a poem of Sophie's which Marguerite has framed and hung on the wall.

We are in the main bedroom now, and as we pass the ornate mantelpiece, Marguerite stops to look at a photograph of Sophie. It is the familiar one, widely published in the newspapers after her death, and taken from her passport and her *carte d'identité*. Her hair is swept back and her face looks drawn; like all passport photographs, it does not do its subject justice. Marguerite looks at it and says that Sophie talks to her at night. Suddenly behind me I hear sobbing. I turn. Georges has burst into tears. Marguerite leads me out of the room by the arm. We leave her husband to his grief, not because we want to abandon him in a moment of need but because that is the way he prefers it. We return to the *salon* and await his return.

Later in the evening Bertrand calls in. Marie Madeleine told me in advance that Sophie's brother talks very little about the tragedy and I understand this. Different people have different ways of dealing with such awful events. Bertrand is classically handsome in a French way, and is quiet-spoken and extremely gracious and polite. We eat a beautifully cooked dinner accompanied by red wine and followed by an array of cheeses. Marguerite, like any good Irish mother, insists that I have second helpings, and who could spurn such hospitality? Later, Bertrand walks with me up the road to the intersection where we say goodnight, until the morning when we are to meet again. I walk in the cool night air towards the Louvre and the Seine. It must have been a walk Sophie took many times and I would suspect that she never lost that sense of wonder that this part of Paris evokes; it reeks of culture and history and romance.

I reach the pedestrian bridge and, looking back towards the Louvre, I get a flashback of an experience that had not entered my consciousness for many years. As a young teenager I had trooped outside the magnificent façade of the gallery for one or two days as a special extra in a British film shot entirely in Ireland, except for this one exterior scene.

The film, entitled *Term of Trial*, was based on a book called *The Burden of Proof*, and starred my boyhood hero Terence Stamp and the wonderful French actress Simone Signoret. It was a marvellous way to be introduced to Paris, the city of dreams. I thought of my naïvety and innocence then and how the years had unfolded with knowledge, experience, love, heartbreak and horror.

I remember a picture of Sophie about the same age as I was then, the shining essence of innocence, her blonde head turned slightly to the right, her lovely brown eyes directed straight at the lens, surrounded by a constellation of freckles. This was her city, her teenage space. Here she was full of hope, looking forward to her future, dreaming her dreams as all young people do.

The following morning I walk back from the hotel to the Bouniol apartment, arriving at 9.30am. Bertrand, Georges and Marguerite and myself share numerous cups of tea as we discuss the location and origin of the Bouniol family. Bertrand describes the Lozere region where the family originated.

'Lozere is in south-central France with a very similar landscape to Ireland and is one of the most sparsely populated areas of the country. It is primarily an agricultural community. Clermont Ferrand and Montpellier are the closest big towns, about 170 kilometres from the village where the Bouniols lived. While the countryside is close to Ireland, the people of the region are more like mountain people.

'The winters are very harsh, with snow on the ground for between two and three months every year, so sometimes communications are difficult between places and villages of the region. Therefore families are very important and very close, partly because of the toughness of the mountain terrain. The families and the people of the region are also very loyal and supportive, both on a personal and economic level.'

This confirms every impression I have got of the Bouniols and it deepens the impact of the tragedy. The Bouniols, like the families of their home region and their forebears, are tightly knit. They operate, even after the children have grown up and left the nest, as a unit. How often Sophie would announce to Daniel, 'I must see my family', and off she would go to see her brothers and parents. I have the strong sense of a bonded family, hurt and reduced, but still pulling together.

Just two streets away from the Bouniol apartment was,

for many decades, the location of the biggest market in Paris, where Georges's parents moved in 1924 to open a coffee shop. They lived above the shop. This trade was a tradition of Lozerians and their neighbours from Aveyron and Cantal, who created eighty percent of the coffee shops in Paris – a very important aspect of social life in the metropolis. In time Georges's aunt and uncle would be summoned from Lozere to join the thriving business of serving coffee to the stallholders and traders who thronged the market.

The Bouniols worked very long hours – often a sixteen-hour day. They were hard and diligent workers in the tradition of the region they hailed from. Though living and working in Paris, they would never forget their roots. As the shops expanded, extra staff would be recruited from Lozere. In this way they rivalled the Italians in creating native communities around their businesses. The coffee business thrived and to this day the Bouniols know the descendants of three families who worked for Georges's father, Marcel.

Georges was born in the apartment above the coffee shop on 29 July 1926, just over five minutes walk from where he now lives. The market has long been banished to the suburbs, the coffee shop is gone, but the apartment is still there and he passes the place of his birth almost on a daily basis. Georges attended a local primary school, then high school and eventually university where he studied and qualified in dentistry.

Marguerite's father, Raymond Gazlan, came from Poitiers and was an engineer in charge of rural electrification. He met his future wife, Thérèse Cros, in Lozere where he had moved to work. They married in Montpellier and Marguerite was the first of four children, including Marie Madeleine, Michel and Jean Pierre.

When she had left school, Marguerite moved to Paris where she worked for a company in the city's stock exchange. She met Georges, who was doing his compulsory military service, at a regular social meeting of Lozere people based and working in the city. They were married in 1954. Georges was working with an older dentist in the building in Rue Tiquetonne. He eventually took over the practice and bought the apartment, which housed the business and living quarters, in 1956.

The Bouniols are the type of people who face up to the major decisions in their life and then simply get on with it. They do not have any inherent sense of the dramatic, but the next event in their lives was a source of great joy. Marguerite became pregnant in late October of that year and on 28 July 1957, their first child was born, a girl who was named Sophie Andrée Jacqueline Bouniol.

Georges smiles at the memory, and for a few moments he is back to a time without the shackles of grief. 'She was beautiful and very special, as all children are, but right from the beginning her prettiness and liveliness was special. We called her our cherry blossom.'

Marie Madeleine would later recall: 'Sophie was the most beautiful baby I have ever seen. Absolutely ravishing. I was fascinated by her; even as a baby she had this aura, a light emanated from her presence. She was lovely and most unusual.'

Almost two years later, on 20 April 1959, Bertrand was born, a different bundle of joy. 'Sophie was very energetic and outgoing as a child, while Bertrand was always quiet and shy,' says Marguerite. Once Marguerite's mother wanted a portrait of her grandchild, but Sophie just could not stay still for a minute.

Sophie progressed through primary and secondary school, from an early age displaying an aptitude for literature and languages and showing a great interest in writing. She had no interest in sport.

Bertrand recalls his and Sophie's first introduction to Ireland. 'In July 1971, when Sophie was fourteen and I was about twelve, we went on an exchange programme to a family in Dublin. Their name was McKiernan. They lived in Sutton and as I remember they had a large family. The next month Patricia [McKiernan], who was the same age as Sophie, came over to Paris to stay with our family for a month. We really enjoyed that time.

'The following year I went back to the McKiernan family, but Sophie moved to another family. I think that she really got a feel for the people and the country which later reminded her, especially in rural areas, of the Lozere region and the origins of the Bouniol family,' Bertrand recalls. It was, in its own modest way, the start of Sophie's love affair with Ireland.

Sophie entered her last year in high school and for the latter half of the year her parents sent her to a private Dominican convent school in Rome, where she successfully passed her *Baccalaureate*. She had applied for a place in the University of Paris, and in the autumn of 1975 she enrolled there as a student in a general law course. Bertrand is not quite sure why Sophie chose law, given her avowed interest in literature, but it was a choice that she would acknowledge in a relatively short time to be wrong.

'At this time we were very different in looks and personality. Physically we were opposites – Sophie was blonde and dashing, I was dark-haired and introverted. Sophie was outgoing, got involved in social activities and was interested in the arts. My main interest was in the sciences and I was not very outgoing or a good socialiser. It was as if we were cast from different moulds.

'But we were very close in our minds and our vision and ways of thinking. When we spoke about politics, the family and our outlook on life, our vision was the same. She was always open to other people and their views, even if they did not agree with hers. Sophie was always very interesting because strong, independent-minded people are always more interesting.'

When Bertrand talks of his sister, his words, though restrained and controlled, are tinged with great affection and the subtext of love and admiration is always present. Sophie may well have been different from him, but she was loved all the more for it.

Like her parents, once Sophie made a decision, for good or bad, she got on with it. Within the next three years, she made two major decisions. The first was that she did not like studying law so she dropped out of university, and the second was to marry Pierre, the boyfriend she had met at college. According to Bertrand, she didn't like the university and she found law too dry a subject for her taste. When she dropped out she took different jobs, first selling books, very successfully, and then running a video shop with Pierre. Like everything she was committed to, she threw herself into work with great gusto and energy.

'Sophie could turn her hand to anything,' Marie Madeleine had told me previously. 'She could sell anything. It was not that she was pushy or forward, but she had a very convincing manner that would create interest. She was selling books, but they were very beautiful and, of course, Sophie loved books. Just four weeks after starting in this job, she was running the department. If she liked what she was doing, then she was totally committed.'

It was possibly not the path her parents would have wished her to take, but Sophie had established early on that she was of independent mind and character. One of Georges's forbears had been a teacher, and while formal education skipped a couple of generations, there would have been a reasonable expectation for Sophie to complete an academic course and pursue a professional career. It was what she would eventually settle into, but there were some natural and unpredictable obstacles of life to deal with first.

After the bookselling she and Pierre worked in a video store that was owned by his father. At the tender age of twenty-two they decided to get married. On 21 June 1980, the young couple were married by Pierre's mother's second husband, who was mayor of their village near Orleans. The reception was held in the home of the groom nearby.

Marguerite took out a number of family albums to show me one which contained the wedding photographs. There are stunning portraits of Sophie, a radiant bride, her blonde hair swept back and expertly plaited, reaching down the back of her dress to her waistline. In the church she stands beside Pierre at the traditional spot at the head of the congregation. Summer sunlight pours in through the windows to the couple's right.

Georges, Marguerite, Bertrand, Pascale and other relations look on proudly. Sophie's beauty was more luminous than ever that day. Marie Madeleine constantly tries to capture in words her niece's effect, but she does not have to labour it because here it is, casting her bright spirit up out of the celluloid annals of her life.

Marie Madeleine describes it again: 'Sophie would light up a room, create an atmosphere – vibrant, beautiful but natural and with no sense of pride. She had this aura which was immediately obvious, wherever she went or whatever social or family occasion she attended.'

In another photograph, the church has been replaced by the rectangular room in Pierre's family house where the civil part of the ceremony takes place. Sophie has a smile of pure happiness as she looks across at her mother.

Sophie's whole expression and demeanour in these wedding photographs speak of happiness. Unfortunately, the marriage did not last. Perhaps things happened too quickly for so young a couple, too much responsibility too soon. Sophie became pregnant almost immediately, and on 26 March of the following year, gave birth to her son, Pierre Louis. According to both Bertrand and Marie Madeleine, after the birth the relationship ran into difficulties. They don't know what it was specifically; nothing they were party to. Sophie was not the type of person who would make a family issue of her own problems.

Just months after the birth of their son, Sophie and Pierre separated. They divorced two years later, in 1983. Sophie took Pierre Louis and moved into an apartment near her parents. She worked in a variety of jobs and continued to read voraciously and to write. The family helped out with minding the little boy as he grew up, taking him to school and collecting him, allowing Sophie to earn a living – increasingly in the area of media and public relations work. In the mid-1980s Sophie got a job in the public relations department of Unifrance.

The failure of Sophie's first marriage is not something that the family want to discuss in any depth, naturally enough. Georges and Marguerite have had a long and happy marriage; it is obvious to anyone meeting them that here are two people who sustain and complement each other. They must have hoped for the same good fortune for their daughter in her marriage.

Bertrand said that his sister had a number of relation-ships after the breakdown of her marriage, but the main focuses of her life were Pierre Louis, her career, her family and her friends, the closest being her cousin Alexandra and her work colleague Agnes Thomas. Her circle of friends, Bertrand says, was built up in the period between her sepa-ration from Pierre and her marriage to Daniel, unlike Ber-trand himself whose adult friends originated from school and college.

According to Marie Madeleine, Sophie was very loyal to her close friends, and was very concerned and caring. 'If any of her friends was in difficulty, she would forget herself, drop everything and concentrate on helping where she could. If I – as a mother often does with her daughters – had a problem with Alexandra, Sophie would always act as mediator and the problem would be solved. She was always protecting her friends, especially in work situations – her friends were more important than the job. Her nature was as glowing as her looks. Her politics were more radical than her parents' because Georges and Marguerite are of conservative background and, of course, Sophie's generation were more liberal and more left-wing, promoting individuality of thought.

'This naturally led to friction, especially with Marguerite. They are both independent and strong-minded. An argument would develop on the phone, a big disagreement. Sophie would end the conversation by slamming the phone down. Maguerite might not hear from her for a number of days, but it was always Sophie who picked up the phone and restored relations, because, irrespective of her views and the different world that she occupied and different people that she mixed with, her family were really important to her. If there was a falling-out, it would not last long – she made sure of that. The phone would ring, Marguerite would pick it up and this bright, cheery voice would say, "Hello, this is Sophie." She never let pride interfere with the love for her family.'

Bertrand says that Sophie divided her world of friends,

family and work colleagues into three separate circles, some of which intersected. He drew a simple diagram on a sheet of paper to illustrate what he meant.

The first circle he labelled FAMILY: Pierre Louis, Daniel, Marguerite, Georges, Marie Madeleine, Bertrand, Stephane, Alexandra. The second circle was FRIENDS: Agnes Thomas, Jean Marc Peyron and many other personal friends. The COLLEAGUES circle included Jerome and Catherine Clement from the Arte Channel, Maurice Pialat, André Rousselet, founder and former chief executive of Canal+, Nicholas Seydoux, and Vincent Roget, producer of her films.

And Sophie had a special effect on her friends. After her death, a friend was quoted in the French newspapers as saying: 'She illuminated my existence. She was an archae-ologist of the flesh and passionate about genealogy. She was a woman who was at once very serious and good-humoured, cultivated but incapable of pedantry, honest and always keeping a good rhythm to her life. She was a true artist who inspired confidence. The last time I saw her, she was wear-ing an astonishingly low neckline for a modest woman, she looked incredibly sexy.'

Irrespective of their different worlds, her family and friends recognised in Sophie a woman of rare physical and spiritual beauty. The standard she set for herself in any endeavour, personal or professional, she demanded of others.

She was generous and loyal and successful in most things in her life, although her relationships with men could be problematic. And that probably had something to do with those same high standards.

Many close to her say that she also had a mysterious side to her, the part of Sophie that she did not allow anyone else to know, the enigmatic compartment to which only she had access. Some of the photographs of her, like the one taken in the garden at Ambax, show her in deep, pensive mood, but who could know what was going on in her mind? It was a mind, if judged by her library, that was deep and constantly curious.

Chapter Seven

SOPHIE – IN HER OWN WORDS
'I feel at ease here'

Sophie Toscan du Plantier's family very kindly gave me a section from her diary relating to her search for the house in West Cork. We have translated it here. It gives us a privileged insight into her feelings and thoughts, and her first images of the place she came to love.

[Missing words or those appearing in brackets are as written by Sophie; she may have heard the name of a location, for example, Beara, but not known how to spell it, so wrote it as it sounded to her.]

'I think a lot about the house in Ireland; Daniel has told everybody, and people are happy for me!

'I am going to go there very soon with Alexandra. We will visit the southwestern and western regions to see which area I would prefer and also to get some information on prices.

'Will I be able to tolerate the solitude of a country like Ireland? Certainly it is similar in that way to Lozere. I would like a place among the heathland, just like at l'Aubrac, with the sea nearby, and write there, in that noisy and windy tranquillity. I would like to go there out of season, to settle in for the winter and autumn; to move in there under the gaze of everyone.

'I don't know if it's a good idea to go over there, thinking about the views of others on my crazy enterprise. Well, we will see! I have always dreamed of putting down roots in a country like that! But why would I want to *find* a country? I already have one. But I am looking for another that would be *mine*, that I would make my own, somewhere I would be happy and that would be happy to have me.

'Yesterday we visited two houses; one smaller than the other. The larger of the houses is situated in a very wild, very beautiful corner of the country, but it's a rather strange house: two rooms downstairs, three rooms upstairs: a little bleak, but with potential for renovation.

'I have to step back a little. I have such a vision of Ireland; when I close my eyes I see a countryside of mountains, sea, bogs, and other combinations of features; everything changes so quickly here: the scenery, the vegetation, nature! Everything goes by so quickly. Travel a few kilometres distance in the car and you are in another country! With my habitual slowness, I have trouble keeping up with it.

'Today we visited a lot of houses, but none that were really in a wild place; they were always within sight of other houses, and of designs that fitted into the landscape with varying degrees of success.

'I do want neighbours, but not to be able to see them; tomorrow we will go to (les … Boven) and we will see lots of other places.

'The people are genuinely very nice, very obliging and somewhat amused to see two young French women coming to choose a house!

'We even made a visit to an island this evening: the 'Island of Bears' [*probably Bere Island, off Castletownbere, County Cork*]; a very pretty island, but the house was situated right beside an army barracks. So that didn't tempt me; even if it was an Irish army barracks!

'We leave Kenmare and go towards (Les "Bure …"). A long walk awaits us. If I don't find a house on this trip, I must at least make a choice as to the region that suits me best.

'For the past three days we have kept up a hellish pace: six hours in the car on fairly small roads with deep potholes in the flooded crossroads, which lead us to houses that are, in theory, for sale; it must be admitted that the majority of them are rather disappointing: the environment is never really isolated, and the nearby houses are not always very pretty. The most pleasing place we saw was (le "…")

'So, lots of driving and nights in rather chilly Bed and Breakfasts. It took us a long time to get going in the mornings because the roadways were so cold.

'Everything is working out well with Alexandra, who has caught on to the system and the fact that we are not on holiday. She has become more and more considerate and full of information.

'Often the farmhouses make their own bread. It is good bread, brown and nourishing; a real treat, almost a cake.

'The Irish love their country in a more exclusive way than the Lozerians. They possess an almost touching, solicitous love of their country; they even warn us about its drawbacks, in case we would be disappointed with it.

'It is a country of endurance, of resistance, pride in a flag, more than mere roots! There is, simultaneously, pride and concern in the attachment of an Irishman to his country; no resignation, despite the clarity of their thoughts, their sayings and their proverbs. They speak earnestly and with great interest about the weather and constantly assure us that the weather we are having today is not normal – it must be said that it is very cold at the moment.

'I really love this country; I am adapting to it, and at the same time my body is, more or less, getting used to the cold; I am becoming hardened to it and I feel at ease here, with the people, their language and their thoughts.

'To adapt oneself to a country and a people you must also follow the same rhythm, with the same easiness and kindness; I would love to find a house and to stay there for a time. Perhaps it doesn't need to be too isolated for me to find serenity. [*Translator's note: Sophie had an ideal notion of what she wanted in a house – somewhere in a very isolated and untamed environment that would provide a retreat where she could write and be peaceful, but after seeing a lot of houses, she is coming to realise that it may not be possible to find exactly what she wants, so she is saying that maybe she can achieve the serenity and calm she craves in a house that isn't quite as isolated as she originally planned. This would explain why she ended up in a house that, while isolated, did have neighbours.*]

'The scenery is to die for; it changes all the time, going from English-type countryside with Swiss-chalet-like houses, to stony desert and red dust.

'Sometimes stands of fir trees appear on the horizon, but rarely; trees grow badly here. To protect themselves from the wind, the people have built small stone walls, which don't create too much resistance to the wind and therefore don't collapse too quickly. From a distance they look like lacework, with the sky and the sun showing through the stones.

'Tomorrow we are going to John Casey's, a property and insurance agent. We wait there while he goes in search of the key of a house that we want to view again. I like this area, and the choice I must make between the two houses that I prefer is also a choice between two climates; on the one hand, a gentle climate, sweet scenery and a house that is not so pretty; on the other there is a more isolated house on the cliffs above rocks, a strong and windy landscape, where the sky and the sea share the horizon; a more comfortable house. [*This is the house in Toormore that Sophie bought.*]

'Well, much good that has done me; I have two houses, and I don't know which one to choose! It's impossible! I saw them both again today and I still didn't succeed in making up my mind.

'Which one should I pick? It's difficult to choose between gentleness and force, the grandiose and the plain, cliffs and rocks! I don't know; I will have to take some time to see which one comes back to me most often in spirit. I need some time and some distance to think about it, to decide on what I want without taking too much notice of my vanity or or my pride. As I have taken pains to convey, I will have to dig out that side of my personality.

'Tonight we got a puncture. I was trying to keep to the left side of the road; suddenly there were two big stones, one after the other, and my tyre was gone! It was a stormy night and we were in the middle of the mountains. An Irishman passed us by and he had us repaired in exactly six minutes; Bravo to that unknown Irishman!

'Returning to Paris after a very tiring week, I have pains in my back and kidneys, undoubtedly from the car – I will have to drink a lot. But I also bring back with me a lot of pleasant memories!

'Ireland: the sky and the sea and the land, as far as the eye can see. Furrows in the earth from cutting and harvesting the turf; autumn when everything is red and green like the hair and the eyes of the Irish people; every description seems to me to be inadequate to capture the reality of the country.'

Chapter Eight
THE HUSBAND'S STORY

I met Daniel Toscan du Plantier by appointment in the Bouniol family apartment near the Louvre in Paris on 3 July 2002. There had been no arrangement yet on his part to co-operate with the book, as he had, in common with the rest of the family, taken a decision some years previously not to talk to the press about his wife's murder. Earlier, while researching an article for the *Sunday Independent*, I had made numerous attempts to contact him at the Unifrance headquarters, but my calls were never returned.

I was also aware that Daniel had become embroiled in some controversy over the investigation and had been reported as criticising it. I worried too that the meeting might turn into a stand-off because Sophie's former husband had since moved on into another relationship, which resulted in marriage and a child.

I was aware that he and Sophie had split up a number of times during their marriage, and that on one occasion she arrived to stay at the West Cork house with another man. This must have been difficult for everybody.

When I was getting ready to meet Daniel, Sophie's father, Georges, told me he wanted me to ask Daniel why he had decided to marry Sophie. It may seem a strange request, but I assumed that he simply needed to be reassured that his beloved and cherished daughter had been loved in her marriage, even if it had had difficulties. Nevertheless, it was a question I was uncertain about putting to Daniel Toscan du Plantier, especially on a first encounter.

Despite these anxieties, I was looking forward to meeting Du Plantier. I had heard so much about him and read some disparaging reports, which I could see were written on the thinnest of good source knowledge.

He arrived into the living-room of the apartment at about 6.00pm, a tall, imposing figure of a man who, of course, had aged since the photographs I had seen of him had been taken; I particularly remembered two striking ones with himself and Sophie, Pierre Louis and his son Carlo, at the 1990 Cannes festival – Daniel wears a traditional tuxedo while Sophie, her hair tied back, wears a simple but elegant black dress, and looks radiant. In the background there is a phalanx of television news cameras, banked on a platform, getting the personalities and celebrities on their way into the Palais. Another photograph is a night-time shot of Daniel with a very wide grin and Sophie laughing almost uproariously, as if someone has just cracked a damn good joke. If anyone were to ask me if these presented portraits of a happy couple, I would without the slightest hesitation answer in the affirmative. They have all the appearance of a couple in love, and the glamorous surroundings only seem to emphasise rather than detract from their happiness.

Our opening conversation concerns the murder and the seemingly remote possibility of it ever being resolved. Daniel says that, contrary to reports, he never criticised the police investigation, but rather the legal system in Ireland, which requires such a burden of proof even to get to trial, never mind succeeding in court; and this allows the killer to go unpunished after all this time. For the family this is a source of frustration, humiliation and even anger. Each year that passes makes the possibility of justice seem more and more remote, while the pain caused by the murder goes on and on.

The complete absence of DNA evidence is a mystery to him too, he says. We discuss the psychological make-up of the killer and his actions and intentions in an apparently motiveless attack. I pass on the information that the expert investigators and profilers have assembled on the personality and motivation of such killers. And then there is the sheer luck that has helped him evade being brought to trial. Apart from having had the time and opportunity to dispose of the evidence, it is incredible, I remark to Daniel, that not one spot of his flesh or blood has been found, either on the second murder weapon or on the barbed wire and briars that entrapped his victim.

'Is it possible that there has been no progress because such a high-profile case would damage the image of West Cork and consequently the tourist trade?' Daniel asks. 'It is something we have discussed in the family as a possibility, because we can find no other obvious logic.' I explain that no such theory in relation to the tourist trade has arisen and that, in fact, the greater damage is the fact that the case has *not* been brought to a conclusion and that the killer is still at large in the area. If the area is unsafe, with a maniac lurking, waiting for the opportunity to kill again, then the notion that Ireland is a country where justice is in short supply must be in everyone's mind. However, the police investigation has stood the test of an independent review and a further, substantial file has been sent to the DPP.

There has been a plethora of articles in the French media, such as *Le Figaro* and *Paris Match*, pointing an accusing finger at the investigation, the police, the Irish legal system. We ponder these and talk the circles that have been traversed for years by the murder investigators and all those affected by the crime, in France, in Ireland and elsewhere, and in particular those closest to Sophie. We reach the same conclusion of disbelief and despair that nothing has progressed. Is there some insurmountable difficulty we don't know about? What could it be? We go back to talking of Sophie.

'I met Sophie first shortly after I was elected chairman of Unifrance in 1988. She had been working in the press relations department and she had a problem with a manager, and I had a talk with her about how to resolve the problem. I quickly found out that she had no intention of following my advice. She could not work with this person and that was final. Without prejudice I told Sophie that despite the excellence of her work that she would better off leaving Unifrance to pursue an independent career.

'At first she interpreted my opinion as a way to get rid of her and favour the other person who would remain on in the organisation, and was angry. But I had other ideas and genuinely believed that Sophie had the ability to become an independent producer. We worked together in Cannes and I think that possibly she was still angry with me about the other matter, but we did attend functions together. She was serious about her work and did not seem to be over-impressed by the whole Cannes way of doing business – but that is the film way of doing things, all over the world, not just Cannes, which, of course, has this big reputation.'

At that time Daniel was in the process of separating from his second wife, the actress and director Francesca Comencini, and when he and Sophie returned to Paris by car, with Sophie's friend Agnes Thomas, they spent a long time discussing their situation on the phone.

'I think Sophie was still furious about the Unifrance

situation, but the basic fact was the manager did not like her and she hated him. There was no possibility of them continuing. She told me that she did not want to spend time with me and that she had to make her choice.'

Despite her reservations, just one month later they were spending time at Daniel's country home in Ambax and then started living together. But Sophie had firm ideas of what her status should be, as Daniel had a reputation with women that went before him.

'Although I was separated, Sophie told me unequivocally that she would not continue to live with a married man. You are too visible, have too high a profile, she told me, and added that she had no intention of being known as the mistress of a film producer. She was very independent-minded, she looked like an angel but had a volcanic character, she would fight her corner, which is fair enough.'

Sophie was clearly setting out her stall, and while marriage was not on Daniel's mind, he photocopied the lawyer's file on his separation and sent it to Sophie's mother, Marguerite, as proof to Sophie that he intended going through with the divorce. Daniel said that Mrs Bouniol wrote back and said that although he had a bad reputation, her daughter was old enough to make up her own mind. They later decided to get married, the news of which prompted one of Sophie's relatives to burst into tears.

But Sophie was thirty-three years of age, highly

intelligent and independent, and her husband-to-be was nearly fifty, with a great deal of worldly experience. It could not be described as a rash decision. Sophie was certainly, despite her elfin beauty, a far cry from the high-profile actresses that had occupied the producer's bed. Her roots were rural, in Lozere, not in the dizzy heights of French theatre or Italian film, a circus in which, in common with the rest of the media and film world, it is notoriously diffi-cult to maintain a relationship. Her parents too lived in a world of pragmatism, not in some transient illusory world.

But when Sophie made up her mind, that was that. It was a characteristic that her companions and lovers had long recognised. She had hesitated in the start, wanting to be sure, but when she saw that Daniel had conceded to her demands – no mean feat given the power and charm of the man – she decided to go ahead.

'I think the fact that I had such a high profile and reputa-tion in the film industry did inhibit her at first, because she was not that type of person who wanted to be in the lime-light and for me it was part of the job, almost second nature; it made Sophie feel uncomfortable. She was also quite pos-sessive and wanted any ties I had left to Francesca com-pletely cut, which is something that I was not used to, but understood. When I think of it, we got married quite quickly.'

It was just a year after they began their relationship and

the ceremony was performed by Sophie's mother, Marguerite, in June 1990, in her capacity as deputy mayor of Paris's second *arrondissement*. It was a simple affair compared with her first marriage. Instead of the long, flowing wedding dress, Sophie wore an elegant black jacket and a simple white dress. Her hair was tied back. Daniel dressed in a sober, blue, pinstriped suit and in the photographs they wear expressions of restrained joy – they are adults, after all, and know that only fairy stories and Jane Austen novels end with the lovers marrying and living happily ever after.

Marguerite Bouniol later said that she was sorry that she had performed the ceremony, adding: 'Maybe it brought them bad luck.' It is a case of the mother being too hard on herself. Apart from Sophie's death, when luck and God had taken a holiday, the couple, in their individual ways, both professionally and personally, were people who created their own luck. Daniel had an incredible body of work behind him as well as several relationships, and Sophie was about to give an indication of her true potential in creative terms. That potential had probably been postponed by her early marriage and the responsibility of bringing up Pierre Louis, so it now made her twice as focused on grasping every opportunity that offered itself.

Sophie was not just embarking on a new marriage but a new direction in her career, a difficult enough balancing act. Daniel had encouraged her to set up as an independent film producer, having seen that potential in her determination, ability to organise, refusal to be overwhelmed by the odds and willingness to take risks. Those qualities cannot be taught, they are innate, though perhaps accentuated by her family background. And she had a passion for everything she did.

'We set up a company and I gave her an office in a complex which housed my film production and record company, Erato Films and Erato Records. But she was fiercely independent and did most of the establishing work herself with the vice chairman of the Arte channel, Jerome Clement, who she was very close to. She was very careful to keep a professional distance from me, because whatever she was to achieve she wanted to prove she could do it without help. She wanted to prove herself in the medium and she did.'

As a fledgling producer Sophie made life more difficult for herself by choosing what could be considered esoteric subjects, which, in this time of mass-produced television, are very difficult to finance and sell on.

'They were,' remarks Daniel, 'very ambitious and cultural films, about Greek dance, African art and the French idea of cinema. But Sophie would get obsessed with the subject and put in tremendous energy and time on the development, working day and night, making sure that the film would happen. She never let the difficulties she encountered in having the film financed get in her way or bring her down. She had that self-belief that drives all good film-makers, and the intensity of drive to make them happen.'

While Jacques Chirac was Mayor of Paris, Sophie and Daniel were invited to a private dinner in the Hotel de Ville. Chirac enquired about Sophie's work and she told him that she was working on a film about African art and he asked when it would be broadcast. Some time later, when Chirac had been elevated to the role of President of France, he sent a fax to Sophie telling her how much he had enjoyed the programme. High praise indeed, but such flattery, however genuine, would never go to Sophie's head. And she avoided any self-publicity like the plague.

'She wanted to be recognised for her talent, not by her looks or self-promotion. I had a friend who wanted to do a story on us for *Paris Match*. I had my children with me, but Sophie just fled the house. She would have nothing to do with the article. She said that I would pay for this some day. She was right, because after she died, those photos were everywhere, without her.'

In private, however, she did sit for the camera, particularly on family occasions and with her beloved Pierre Louis. But even in those photographs the times when she stares directly at the lens are very rare.

Some of Daniel's favourite photographs were taken at the country house in Ambax. In one, Sophie reaches towards a wall of ivy, her magnificently plaited hair reaching right down her back. In another she sits in a chair in the garden. She wears a blue floral dress and her head is tilted towards the ground, her eyes fixed in a thoughtful stare. The shadows of the branches are painted in the background by the summer sunlight. It is an enigmatic picture, inviting the viewer to wonder what is going on in the subject's mind.

Daniel freely admits that there were aspects of Sophie's personality that mystified him and that still do until this day. And the marriage had been rocky at times. 'Yes, we did have our problems,' he says, 'but tell me what relationship does not have its troubles? We were no different. We did have a number of separations, but in the end we had worked things out. Sophie could be impulsive, if she was not happy the way things were, she would just disappear. Sometimes I did not know where she had gone and after a while it became a bit of a joke between us.

'Once we had a disagreement and she went back to her own apartment in the ninth *arrondissement* for two weeks. She was a very strong character. She arrived back one day, but there was a very intense and tough discussion before Sophie agreed to move back in with me.

'I remember, during one period of separation, I was having a four-storey house on Rue de Marie renovated and Sophie insisted, because she had wanted to get involved before our falling out, that she come into the house every day and supervise the renovation and decoration. And it was no easy task, because the job entailed a complete transformation. Sophie decided everything, from the architect to the furnishings, and saw the new house being created. It gave her great pleasure. "I will make this house for you," she told me. We had disagreed, but she was not one to bear a grudge. That was a very appealing and generous quality which made up for her impulsiveness.

'Sometimes it had nothing to do with a disagreement when she would go away. She might spend weeks writing at our country house. Then she seemed to get uneasy and unsettled and would just turn around to me and say, "I must go to my parents. I have to see my family. I will see you when I come back." And she would just go.

'She did have a capacity to break off relationships suddenly. She had a mystical idea of love – very demanding. She was not a person to have casual affairs, she was easily disappointed. She wanted a spiritual absolute. This is very difficult to live up to.'

As a devotee of WB Yeats, the pull between the ideal and the real, theory and practicality, love and hate, the joy of involvement and the delight in escapism, would have intrigued Sophie. She had high ideals of love, and a fear of disappointment, just like her literary hero did. The mystical life was at the centre of everything Yeats did and wrote about; he was like a man who is always seeking 'infinite feeling, infinite battle, infinite repose'. Sophie – by all accounts a perfectionist with an intense creative drive – was also true to her emotions and fearful of compromise. Such a pursuit of perfection, by its very nature, causes difficulties.

Sophie could be said to have had the world at her feet. Marriage to a charismatic and powerful man, regular international travel, a magnificent townhouse in the city, a lovely house in the country, mixing in the highest social circles in Paris. She had access to wealth and to the most fashionable clothes and restaurants. To top it all off, she was beautiful. She was in a position that most women dream of but never attain, a firmament reserved for the privileged few. And yet, after a domestic row, she could disappear, sometimes to the house of Marie Madeleine in Geneva. She also had a need to escape all this glamour in the most fashionable city in the world by searching for a retreat in one of the wildest and most remote parts of Ireland.

Sophie was not enamoured of the glitz and hype that accompanied the film festivals which Daniel had to attend in his capacity as head of Unifrance.

'Sophie accompanied me to Cannes,' he explained, 'and though she was not excited or stimulated by film society, she always came along in the end. She would tell me before we set out for Cannes: "Daniel, I am staying for three days, no longer." Inevitably she stayed the whole ten days and I think she enjoyed the festival. She also accompanied me on many promotional tours. She resisted at first, because she did not like the publicity aspect of the trips – cameras flashing constantly, rounds of receptions, parties, screenings and discussions – but I think, in the end, she was more tolerant of my social obligations.'

Nonetheless, when Sophie told her husband about her interest in acquiring a house in Ireland, Daniel says, 'I supported the idea, and after Alexandra and Sophie had travelled to Ireland hunting for the house the choice had come down to two, one near the sea and the other in an isolated area. It was the second one that she chose. I did not like the idea of her staying in such remoteness alone, but, looking back, Sophie had no concept of the risk.

'When she operated as an independent producer from my office complex she never displayed any sense of danger, although it was located in a tough northern suburb of Paris where there was a lot of drug-taking and violence. I always thought it was unsafe, but Sophie believed that she had the strength to deal with whatever situation transpired. She never considered the possibility that she might be under threat. I was always worried about her, especially if she was working late. It was a strange place, a little like parts of London. She would go regularly and have coffee alone in this very tough neighbourhood, more than likely sitting next to drug dealers. When I objected, she said I was just displaying bourgeois prejudice to the people of a less well-off area.'

Daniel says, without a hint of criticism but simply as a matter of fact, that Sophie was ambitious, strong-willed and difficult. Not surprisingly, most people of such character kick over the traces, do not accept fools gladly and challenge the convention of easy acceptance. Life is not about sitting back, but about mounting a challenge to yourself and, in consequence, to others. And if such people are difficult, they are also exceptional and that is a description that nobody has denied Sophie Bouniol.

'Yes, certainly she loved a challenge and was intense about everything that she did,' her husband recalls. In between productions she was always writing, mostly at Ambax, a place she loved because it was rural and the country people were straightforward and simple and down-to-earth. There she wrote poems, novels, short stories. Sophie worked hard, all the time.

'At our country house, when she would go there alone to write, she would often take walks in the woods in the middle of the night. That is something that I would never do. But once Sophie had that mindset there was no point in trying to talk her out of it. I really believe she had no sense of danger. She loved Ireland and in particular the countryside of West Cork. Its wild beauty and isolation held a great appeal for her and she loved the people, who she had absolutely no reason not to trust.'

After Sophie acquired the house in Dunmanus West,

which Daniel paid for, she withdrew more, but not altogether, from the film social rounds. She would visit the house, of which Daniel says she was intensely proud, two or three times a year, always with relatives or friends and once with Daniel.

'I paid for it, yes, but I was not excited by the idea of the house and its location, far too out of the way and not a place a woman should stay alone. I always had that feeling for the years up to Sophie's death. You think about it now, but what can you do? Sophie considered West Cork one of the safest places in the world. But there are crazy people everywhere.

'She always went with friends or relatives – Alexandra, Pierre Louis, Carlo or Georges and Marguerite. Therefore there had been no real test of my reservations about going there alone, until the last time, of course. Even though I had paid for the house, it was Sophie's and she loved to go there and bring people to stay. That was the extent to which she was attached to it and the measure of her love and commitment to the area. She never felt in the slightest vulnerable in Dunmanus West. She had never been given the slightest reason to have any fear of anyone.'

I suggest to Daniel that it was this very reason – her lack of vulnerability; her refusal to see anything bad about the hous,e or the area, despite Alexandra's sixth sense – that made her perfect prey for the killer. Suspicion was not part of her visits to Ireland. There is enough suspicion and infighting and back-biting in the film and television business to fill Toormore Bay; it was to escape what she described as her 'multi-storey' life in Paris that she came to West Cork.

According to Daniel their married life was happy and stable, and they had not been separated for two years before her last fateful journey. Things had been going so well between them that Sophie had expressed the desire to have another child. They had discussed the matter at length and had agreed to go ahead. Sophie's preference was for a baby girl, who would be named Thérèse.

'Yes, things had been going well; we lived a normal, daily life. Sophie avoided the social functions, or what she considered the jetsetters' life. She was working hard at her films and becoming successful and recognised, and always continued to write. She had the outlet of the house in Dunmanus West and was becoming more self-fulfilled and still maintaining her independence of mind. There were many rumours after Sophie's death that our marriage was in difficulties and that we were going to divorce. This was not true.'

Sophie's family confirm this, and the fact that Sophie had intended to have a child with Daniel. Just a day or two before she left for Ireland, Sophie visited Bertrand's wife, Pascale, in a Paris maternity hospital to see her newborn nephew. There she told her sister-in-law of her plan to have another child. Clearly, Sophie was far more relaxed and happy in her marriage now, and there was no suggestion that having the child was an attempt to shore up a crumbling relationship.

So, where did the false rumours of a troubled marriage emanate from? They were another part of the misinformation circulating immediately after the tragedy, during which stories of the marriage split-up seemed to support the common practice of considering the husband as a prime suspect in the murder of a wife.

Of course, Daniel, as well as the rest of Sophie's family, was interviewed and eliminated from police enquiries. But in the interim, false rumours successfully deflected attention from the real killer, so successfully that it became 'fact' in print that the couple were having marital problems. The media bought it, and so did I at the time.

Daniel talks revealingly and frankly about the planned-for new baby. He tells me that in the months leading up to Sophie's final journey to West Cork, Sophie had become obsessed about having a child and that they made love often during that time, with Sophie always checking to make sure that she was at the optimum stage to become pregnant.

At the end of November and beginning of December 1996, Daniel and Sophie had travelled to a film festival in Acapulco. 'It was a long trip,' explained Daniel. 'The weather was hot and there was an incessant round of receptions and parties, and when we returned to Paris we were very tired. The trip back was exhausting, with the added factor of jet lag on top of the tiredness. Afterwards, Sophie had to finish off a film. Then she learned that there was a problem with the heating in the house in Ireland. She decided she would go to West Cork, sort out the problem, but also take a bit of time out, read and relax.'

In her typical fashion, Sophie did not tell Daniel the precise day of her return; it was a form of independence but also a tease – she would say that she would go for a finite time and then often extend her stay. Sophie wanted company, but when it did not transpire, she decided to go on her own. According to Daniel, she was happy enough to do that and displayed no fear or sense of premonition. Other family members disagree.

'On Thursday evening, 19 December, we attended a party in *Les Bains Douches*, a well-known Paris club. Even though Sophie was beginning to feel that she was becoming a jet-setter, she entered the spirit of the evening and was very positive. She spent some hours having an intense, passionate conversation with a film-maker. It was a typical creator's discussion about ideas. Sophie was in sparkling form and looked radiant. It was a very pleasant evening, which everyone present enjoyed thoroughly. It was Christmas and we were all looking forward to the break and to be with our families.'

The following morning, Sophie left their Paris house and headed off to the airport to catch a lunchtime flight to Cork. Daniel got no sense of anything strange, although it did concern him that Sophie was staying alone in Dunmanus West for the first time. It had been something that bothered him from the first time that his wife had made her choice of holiday home. But he knew better than to make it a big issue. He did, in a gentle way, try to persuade her not to go. But Sophie was going, and now she was gone. They had agreed to talk on the phone about their Christmas arrangements. Sophie was not sure of the exact day of her return, so she had purchased two tickets back to Paris – one for 23 December and the other for the following day, Christmas Eve.

Daniel was the last person to talk to Sophie. On the fateful night, around midnight, they had a long discussion about a variety of things.

'It was a very jovial, relaxed discussion,' recalls Daniel. 'I said that it would be nice to have my wife home for Christmas, but Sophie teased me in her typical way. She said: "Daniel, I love to be alone, perhaps I will stay on here and study and read." She then debated what sort of gift she would buy me.'

Later, it would turn out that Sophie had already organised her Christmas gift to her husband. She had telephoned the family gardener at Ambax to order a linden tree for

Daniel. It was to be planted outside their bedroom window.

Daniel continues, 'She was quiet-spoken but, I thought, in very good form. There did not seem to be anything on her mind, or any indication that she felt under threat or fear of any kind.

'Sophie could be comfortable while alone, which a lot of people could not bear. She probably thought the house in Dunmanus West no different than our country house where she spent much time alone. I asked her when she was planning to return home. She had reservations for two days, but could not at that time make up her mind which one, but she said she would definitely be back for Christmas Day. We had a nice conversation, which I think lasted about an hour. It finished about 1.00am.'

The impact of Sophie's death among the film community was immense.

'It was very upsetting; the tragedy was too much for many of my colleagues. The film-maker who had such an intense discussion with Sophie at the party in Paris on the night before she departed for Ireland has never spoken to me since. I think he just cannot bear to experience the emotion and grasp the reality of what happened. Nobody ever imagines that it happens to their friend or relative, but to Sophie ... it was inconceivable that such a bright, talented, ambitious and beautiful woman could suffer this fate. Nobody could speak of it without emotion.'

Legendary French film director Maurice Pialat lived next door to the Toscan du Plantier country home in Ambax and had become very friendly with Sophie. He was devastated by her death. He expressed his sense of loss to Daniel.

'He told me that had I not been his friend he would not have suffered. "I suffer," he said, "but I do not care." That is why some people cannot bear to mention the death of Sophie. But Pialat did say one thing that perfectly expressed his feelings. He told me that I may have lived with great actresses, but Sophie was the star.'

After hearing of the death of Francois Mitterand in January 1996, Sophie wrote to her great friend, André Rousselet, founder of the French television station Canal+: 'We must not cry about the dead, we must think of them.'

Daniel has to leave; he is due to attend a screening.

* * *

After Daniel has left the room, Georges, who has been present with Marguerite during the interview, asks me if I thought that Daniel loved Sophie. A father in this terrible situation needs reassurance that his daughter had some measure of happiness. To people of the Bouniols's generation, the failure of a marriage would be a major event, a loss of status, even a stigma. And Sophie had already had one marriage break-up.

Sophie's own lifestyle would naturally be different from

that of her parents. Her attitude towards institutions, such as marriage, for example, to which she gave short shrift when it did not work, might be difficult for them to comprehend. Daniel had claimed that Sophie was impulsive, but perhaps it was more that she was very decisive?

I am embarrassed to address Georges's question. The straight response is that only two people in the world know the answer, and one is dead. I had not asked Daniel directly – it is not the sort of question you can put to someone you have just met – and indeed you would hesitate making such an inquiry of people you know all your life. But there are certain conclusions one can reasonably draw from the interview and other factors.

There was genuine affection in the way Daniel spoke about Sophie. By his own frank admission, Daniel and his wife had their problems and at one stage during a separation she had a relationship with someone else. For this to happen, it must have been a serious separation – Daniel and everyone else acknowledge that Sophie was not one for casual affairs, she was far too serious about life and love for that.

It must have taken a great deal of commitment on both Daniel and Sophie's part to get over such a separation. It shows that they were prepared to work at their marriage. And in the end there had been no parting for two years. That is a good sign of the stability that had grown between them. Also, there is the fact that I have had confirmation from both Daniel and her family members of Sophie's expressed desire to have a child with Daniel.

Yes, on balance, I say to Georges, I think Daniel did love Sophie.

Part Three

BUILDING A CASE

Chapter Nine

THE INVESTIGATION

'The dead are silenced. It is up to us to give them a voice. We are their voice.'

Murder investigator

Murder investigation is not an exact science. If it were, there would be no unsolved murders and no killers loose among society, unpunished and free to kill again. The investigation of a crime is a human undertaking and is no less fallible than any other endeavour of man. But every investigation follows a certain pre-determined pattern, with meticulously drawn-up procedures, the investigators knowing only too well that any slippage on their part, any carelessness in acquiring or handling evidentiary material could result in disaster in the courtroom. Too many cases have been lost on a technicality.

Today's crime investigators have at their disposal the expertise of forensic scientists and psychological profilers, as well as huge scientific advances in DNA testing, which are helping to solve not just crimes being committed today but unsolved crimes from many years ago. But despite these developments, murderers still walk free. Sometimes what the investigators need, in addition to all the high-tech scientific aids, is simply a lucky break.

Any detective will tell you that one of the most difficult crimes to investigate is a random killing – such as the killing of Sophie Toscan du Plantier. In a random killing there is no obvious link between the victim and the murderer; no outraged husband, battered wife, rejected lover, or known enemy on whom suspicion would automatically fall. It is very difficult to track down the perpetrator of a crime where there is no connection between him and the victim, no obvious motivation. We have only to look at Ireland's recent, sad litany of young women who are missing and presumed dead: Jo Jo Dullard, Annie McCarrick, Deirdre Jacobs for proof of that.

But despite the acknowleged difficulties, the investigation of every murder, random or otherwise, is entered into with the utmost determination on the part of the police to find and bring to justice the person who has flouted the most fundamental commandment: *Thou shalt not kill.* Their search begins at the moment of discovery of the body.

In the case of Sophie Toscan du Plantier, there was a round-the-clock Garda presence at the crime scene from 10.38am on the morning of 23 December 1996 until 6.00pm on 2 January 1997. An incident room was set up at

Bantry Garda Station, the District Headquarters for the area, where Superintendent JP Twomey was in charge of the investigation.

Once they had established the identity of the victim, the Gardaí began to piece together a minute-by-minute account of the movements of Sophie Toscan du Plantier from the time she arrived in Cork Airport on 20 December to the discovery of her lifeless body on the morning of 23 December.

Footage from the security cameras at Cork Airport established that Sophie had disembarked alone from her Paris–Dublin–Cork flight and had set off on her own for West Cork in her hired car. Interviews with her family in France confirmed that none of them had been able to accompany her. Sightings of Sophie in Schull and the surrounding area over the next few days, and statements from the people she had visited, backed up the fact that she was unaccompanied.

Descriptions of Sophie provided by those who knew her in West Cork told of a charming but reserved person who kept to herself, or to the company of family, on her visits to the area. She appeared to be held in high regard and no one could point a finger at anyone living locally who would have had any motive for killing her. In fact, it quickly became obvious that there was no one in West Cork with whom Sophie had the sort of relationship that would hint at an intimate, post-midnight rendezvous in the farmhouse in Dunmanus West.

A log was compiled of all the telephone calls made to and from the house during the period of Sophie's visit. There was nothing unusual there: calls to and from her caretaker, a local tradesman, a woman friend in Paris, Sophie's husband. Interviews with those to whom she had spoken confirmed the innocuous nature, or legitimate purpose of each telephone call.

Checks with the car-hire company, Avis, established the recorded mileage on the Ford Fiesta at the time Sophie picked it up at Cork Airport. The additional mileage clocked up in the following few days corresponded with the various trips around the locality that Sophie had undertaken. There were no unexplained journeys.

Paris Match reported Superintendent JP Twomey as saying: 'We know nothing yet of what happened in the house in Dunmanus between the moment when the victim telephoned her husband on Sunday at 11 o'clock, and the time when her neighbour found her body, on Monday morning at 10.30. What we do know is that Mrs Toscan was brought down at the barrier that borders her property. Murdered by a weapon capable of inflicting wounds, a poker, a tool, a stone, or a piece of wood … we are looking for it. In the house, the lights were off. We found no trace of a struggle, nothing disturbed. The door was locked, it would be impossible for anyone to re-enter as the keys were on the inside of the door ... She had suffered no sexual assault.'

So the question remained: to whom would Sophie have opened her door at such a late hour? Had, as *Paris Match* speculated, someone known to Sophie followed her from France with the intention of killing her? Gardaí checked passenger lists for flights into and out of the country on the relevant dates, as well as passenger movements through the ports, but there was nothing in them that pointed towards a connection with the case.

Of course, the police were aware of the 'impending divorce' and 'tangled love life' stories and of the theories which these had given rise to. Daniel Toscan du Plantier was interviewed at length. He gave his full co-operation and Gardaí came away with a very different picture of the state of the couple's relationship.

With the police now satisfied that French involvement in the murder was highly unlikely, the focus of the investigation concentrated on West Cork. A huge manhunt was underway, with a team of up to forty detectives working full-time on the case. In the days and weeks that followed, the Gardaí distributed and followed up 1,400 questionnaires and conducted exhaustive house-to-house enquiries that stretched all the way around the Mizen peninsula.

'It is very dangerous in any murder investigation to

start with one suspect, or focus on one person. The investigation should start on as broad a base as possible and then narrow down when as much information and statements as possible have been gathered. This is a natural course, and is clearly what happened in this case. It is easy to criticise in retrospect, but police cannot just go out and bring in someone for questioning without good cause,' says a prominent investigator. 'There would have been all sorts of suspects mentioned at the outset of the investigation which is, in essence, a process of elimination.'

As the search in West Cork narrowed, hair samples were taken from a number of people living locally, and clothes were brought away for analysis. Alibis provided for the night of the murder were put under close scrutiny.

The fact that the murder victim's family was in France led to communication problems from early on in the investigation and there were complaints, particularly from Daniel Toscan du Plantier, that the family was not being told anything of what was happening in relation to the investigation in West Cork. Added to this, of course, was the speculation that had appeared in the international press about Sophie's relationships and the state of her marriage.

Daniel had retained the services of a Paris-based lawyer, Paul Haennig, which led to French judge, Brigette Pelligrini, issuing an international *commission rogatoire*, which would enable French police to have access to the information gathered by the Gardaí.

Meanwhile, back in West Cork, the Gardaí had reduced their list of murder suspects. Other persons were suspected of trying to thwart the course of justice by not revealing vital information relating to the murder.

In February 1997 two people – a man and a woman – were arrested in connection with the case and taken to Bandon Garda Station, where they were held under Section Four of the Criminal Justice Act. They were questioned for twelve hours before being released without charge.

A report in the *Sunday Independent* in December 1997 stated that the Gardaí had revealed that 'the murder weapon has never been recovered and a clump of hair found in her hand, which Gardaí believed would identify the perpetrator, turned out to be her own. However, detectives also claim to have built up a substantial body of circumstantial evidence, including an eye-witness account of a man washing a pair of boots in a local river at 4.00am on the morning Sophie's body was discovered.'

One year later, in January 1998 a man was taken in for a second time to Bandon, but was released without charge after the stipulated detention period had elapsed.

At this stage a team of detectives from the National Bureau of Criminal Investigation, led by Detective Chief Superintendent Sean Camon, had joined the West Cork investigating team, now headed by Chief Superintendent Dermot Dwyer.

Daniel Toscan du Plantier, who had not come to Ireland at the time of his wife's murder or immediately afterwards, made a visit to West Cork in July 2000, to be briefed by the Gardaí on the continuing investigation. In a short press conference after the visit, he said he understood that the Gardaí were doing everything possible to bring the case to a conclusion. He said he had been impressed by the quantity and quality of the work that had been done. He was also reported as saying that he believed the Gardaí in West Cork knew the identity of the killer, but he was not at liberty to say what he had been told during the briefing. 'That's the law here. The day I can tell you what I know, the case will be finished,' he said.

Two months after Du Plantier's visit, in September 2000, a nineteen-year-old woman was arrested at a flat in Cork City and taken into Bandon Garda Station for questioning. She was later released. In the same week, Gardaí arrested another woman at a house in West Cork and brought her to Bandon for questioning. She was also released without charge.

A *Sunday Times* report, published on 24 September 2000, spoke of new evidence in the case: 'New information about the death of Sophie Toscan du Plantier … has led to a breakthrough in the investigation.' They reported that two tourists had told Gardaí how they had met a man in a pub less than a year after the killing, and how he had discussed details of the murder with them. The report went on to say that the man 'allegedly discussed the killing at such lengths that the tourists began to feel uneasy. They are understood to have repeated what they were told to Gardaí. But their conversations with him could be little more than pub talk.'

A number of articles published in the French press mention restrictions in the Irish judicial system to explain why the investigation is taking such a long time. In particular, the fact that Gardaí cannot compel suspects to give DNA samples unless they are charged. *Le Monde* of 24 August 2001 quotes Daniel as saying: 'In Ireland, only clear material evidence permits someone to be indicted. *Habeus corpus* does provide big advantages concerning individual liberties, but it also benefits murderers.'

* * *

Why, after such a thorough and long-running investigation, has the case of Sophie Toscan du Plantier remained unsolved? Was the management of the case at fault in any way?

There has been criticism of the way the case was handled, beginning with the undisputed fact that the body was left in the laneway for twenty-four hours before it was examined by the State Pathologist, who was unable to be at the scene of the crime until the morning following the discovery of Sophie's body.

Paul Haennig, the lawyer acting for Daniel Toscan du Plantier, was reported as criticising the early stages of the inquiry. He was quoted as saying that Daniel felt 'nothing positive was happening'.

Obviously, the ideal scenario in any murder case is that the body is examined as near to the time of death as is humanly possible, when the condition of the body and any trace evidence that has been left is in a state where it can tell most about what has happened. The value of a body in forensic and evidentiary terms can decrease dramatically over time, especially if that body is exposed to the elements.

However, external factors, such as the ambient temperature, can also play a part. In warm weather the body changes are speeded up, while in the cold they slow down. The case of murdered civil servant, Marilyn Rynn, who was raped and strangled after getting the bus home to Blanchardstown, Dublin, on 21 December 1995 – almost exactly a year before the murder of Sophie Toscan du Plantier – is a good example of this. Marilyn's body was not discovered for twelve days after she was killed, but during that time the weather was cold and no rain had fallen. DNA evidence, which the murderer had assumed would have disappeared by then, remained preserved.

The air temperature in Toormore on the night after the murder of Sophie Toscan du Plantier was just two degrees above zero. This fact has convinced independent experts that the unavoidably late arrival of the State Pathologist did not have the negative effect on the outcome of the investigation it might have had in other circumstances.

There were also reports that preservation of the crime scene was not all it should have been. In Toormore the crime scene was continually under guard from the time of discovery of the body on 23 December. The body was protected and only touched by a local doctor who examined it and pronounced the victim dead. The pathologist, Dr John Harbison, was the only other person to touch the body.

A former murder investigator, with over three decades of experience and well used to criticism, spoke to me about the critical reports on the case, saying that, normally, the media would be co-operating with murder investigators in the hope that the publicity would encourage information from the public and potential witnesses to come forward.

International criticism of the investigation was such that in December 1997 the case featured in the debates of the Irish parliament, Dáil Éireann. The Minister for Justice, Equality and Law Reform, John O'Donoghue was put under pressure by Deputy Jim Higgins of Mayo. Deputy Higgins wanted to know if a file had been sent to the Director of Public Prosecutions; if so, when, and if charges were to be preferred, when. He outlined the difficulties for the Bouniol family – the wondering, the waiting; difficulties he claimed, that were exacerbated by the the lack of information available. He demanded an apology to the family for the 'insensitive and uncaring manner in which the Department has dealt with this matter.'

In reply, Minister O'Donoghue confirmed that a fax copy of an International Rogatory Commission – a request for mutual assistance in a criminal matter – had been received by the Department on 30 April 1997. The request sought sensitive material in regard to the investigation and the crime. He added that a substantial file had been sent to the Director of Public Prosecutions, and while it was being considered enquiries were continuing. The Minister extended his sympathies to the family of the victim and promised that the case would continue to be pursued vigorously.

On 18 December 1997, Minister O'Donoghue met the Bouniol family in Bantry when they arrived to attend the first anniversary Mass for their daughter.

In France, Judge Pelligrini had authorised the French police authorities to seek permission for members of the force to travel to Ireland to be brought up to date on the case. The judge had written a number of letters to the Irish authorities without receiving a reply. While such a move might be perceived as putting pressure on the Irish side to get something done, it was, for a number of reasons, not least interference in another jurisdiction, doomed to failure. On the most basic of legal tenets, the file on the murder could not be handed over to a third party for fear of prejudicing an upcoming criminal trial.

In February 1998 Deputy Jim Higgins pursued the matter again with Minister O'Donoghue in the Dáil Chamber.

The Minister referred to the meeting that he had had with Marguerite and Georges Bouniol in Bantry. He said that after expressing his deepest sympathy to Sophie's parents he had explained that there would be great difficulty for the Garda authorities in granting a request from the French police authorities for access to the murder investigation file. The Department had sought advice from the DPP and the office of the Attorney General, and had been told that it would not be proper to agree to assist the French authorities, as it was important not to prejudice any subsequent prosecution by premature disclosure of information to third parties.

Mr O'Donoghue said that the DPP, independent in the exercise of its functions, would make a decision in due course. Continuing, he said, 'The investigation into this brutal murder must proceed under Irish law. A basic element of Irish criminal law is that sufficient evidence must be available before a person can be charged and nothing must be allowed to interfere with that process. What we are talking about is an investigation being carried out by the Garda Siochána and every effort being made to bring to justice the perpetrator or perpetrators of this horrific murder.'

At that time a 2,000-page file had been forwarded to the Director of Public Prosecutions. This is, by any standards, a very substantial file. However, no decision was taken to proceed with a prosecution.

Subsequently, an updated file was considered by the DPP, but he ruled that it was, in his view, still insufficient to proceed with a prosecution. Almost six years on, there has been no indication that the DPP will let the case go forward for trial.

This has proved to be a source of great frustration for the family and all concerned. For all the effort and expense involved, there is no result in sight. The embarrassment has been underlined by Daniel Toscan du Plantier's opinion that had the murder taken place in France, it would have gone to court very quickly.

Fresh hope in the case arose recently when minute blood samples taken from particles found on the rear door were sent to Britain and the USA for analysis by a new DNA cross-sampling process. But the results were inconclusive and expectations that the blood might have been from the killer were dashed. It seems the blood was Sophie's.

In 2002 a major review of the investigation was

undertaken by detectives from the Dublin Metropolitan Region Headquarters in Harcourt Terrace. It is believed to have found that at all stages the proper procedures were observed: in the preservation of the scene, in the collecting of evidence and witness statements, the questioning of suspects and in every other aspect of the murder investigation. The review included fresh interviews with some of the witnesses.

The new probe was undertaken with hopes that it could unearth new leads, new evidence, potential evidence that may have been overlooked, or spot contradictions in the mass of witness statements taken to date. However, it is believed that the report has found no major fault with the original investigation, or with the quality or veracity of witness statements. Nor was there any fault found in the method of collection of forensic evidence.

The Garda review is now complete and a report has been sent to the DPP without reference to the original report. But sources close to the investigation are pessimistic about the outcome, simply on the basis that the review had upheld the integrity of the original investigation.

The Gardaí have not, by any means, closed the file on Sophie Toscan du Plantier. They remain determined to explore every avenue in order to solve this case.

Meanwhile the brutal killer is free. If he could get away with murder once, why not again? The grief and pain continues unabated for the Bouniol family, who will once again this December attend the annual memorial service for their beloved Sophie in the tiny village church in Goleen.

And the people of West Cork and Ireland will have to live with the shame of justice not being done for the slaying of a woman who was a guest among them and had put her trust in them.

Chapter Ten

PROFILE OF A KILLER

With the help of forensic psychology experts, former and current murder investigators and a forensic pathologist, a chilling profile of the type of person capable of committing such a murder is put together here. This personality profile and mental map corresponds closely with the profile produced by a top psychologist for the murder investigation team and both assessments are clear in the opinion that the murderer will, given the opportunity, kill again. As one experienced investigator put it: 'This killer is a sadistic beast with psychotic tendencies and perverted sexual urges.'

While profiling is by no means an exact science, forensic psychologists are constantly refining the process, which builds up a mental identikit of the killer, just as a forensic artist would produce a physical identikit to help identify a criminal. And just as this physical representation would fall into categories, such as dark or blonde hair, sallow or pale skin, blue or brown eyes, so psychological profilers can also categorise the mental traits of the killer from a number of sources. Highly accurate personality portraits can be achieved.

The sources used can include post-mortem reports and photographs, the manner and ferocity of the attack, the position of the body; in crimes involving sex, where and how semen was deposited and which parts of the body were interfered with. As Dr Michael Baden, the eminent New York Medical Examiner, puts it, 'The body itself is a crime scene.' In addition, there is the study of transcripts of interviews with suspects, studies of the crime scene, conversations with members of the investigating team and, if the victim has been abducted or the body moved, possible connections between the location and the perpetrator to be explored.

The state of a body can tell a lot about an attacker and whether the killing was random, or rehearsed through fantasy and stalking. If the victim has put up a spirited struggle, the strength of the attacker as well as the age bracket he is likely to fall into can be assessed from the physique of the victim and the injuries he has received.

Injuries to a body can add further details to the portrait of a killer. If the victim has been subjected to humiliation and torture, the nature of the attacker's deviance can be established and profilers can determine if he fits into the category of a killer with psychotic tendencies. There are very few killers in that category who have not previously had some brush with police authorities, usually for offences of a minor nature but connected in some way to a perverse thirst for violence. Educated guesswork and intuition come into play too and, of course, experience of similar cases.

All of these factors contribute to the mental map of a killer, which can be drawn surprisingly quickly and with astonishing accuracy. Top profilers not only utilise the facts available to them, but can also put themselves into the mind of the killer and see the world through his eyes.

The identities of many perpetrators of serious crime – murder, rape, abduction, kidnapping – have been established with the help of profilers. And by pointing investigators in the right direction, profilers have also saved police authorities a huge amount of time and money.

* * *

The science of profiling was developed and perfected in the FBI headquarters at Quantico, Virginia, the setting for Thomas Harris's novel and the film *Silence of the Lambs*. But while profiling is considered a relatively new phenomenon, its roots can be traced back at least to the murder in 1959 of a Kansas farmer, Herbert Clutter, his wife Bonnie, and their children Kenyon and Nancy. by Perry Smith and Dick Hickcock. This gruesome slaughter was controversially and compellingly immortalised in Truman Capote's novel *In Cold Blood*.

The Kansas murders were brutal and apparently without motive. In his confession, Smith described the approach to the isolated farmstead. 'It was the entrance to a private road lined with trees. We slowed down and turned off the lights. Didn't need them. Account of the moon. It was like broad day ... I didn't like the setup; it was almost too impressive.' He constantly refers to the moon and its light coming through the windows of the house, as if it was complicit to the awful events that followed. And there was also constant reference to the lights within the house, as if they illuminated the dark thoughts that raced through his and his accomplice's brains. Everywhere the perpetrators moved, lights were turned on and off until the final victim was silenced.

The ultimate glory for the murderers, though, was having the victims at their utter mercy: captive and absolutely frightened, in a state of abject terror, while the perpetrators were in complete control. And the more the victims pleaded for mercy, the greater was the sense of control.

Many characteristics can be observed from detailed examination of this case and, when compared with other cases, the following general personality traits in a murderer of this type can be inferred:

• He has a paranoid orientation toward the world. He is suspicious and distrustful of others, tends to feel that they discriminate against him, are unfair to him and do not understand him. He is overly sensitive to criticism and cannot tolerate being made fun of. He is quick to sense slight and insult and may misinterpret well-meaning communications.

• He feels a great need for friendship and understanding, but he is very reluctant to confide in others. When he does he expects to be misunderstood, or even betrayed.

• His ability to separate a real situation from his own mental projections is very poor.

• He frequently groups all people together as being hypo-critical, hostile and deserving of whatever he is able to do to them.

• He has an ever-present, poorly controlled rage, easily triggered by any feeling of being tricked, slighted or labelled as inferior by others.

• For the most part, his rage in the past has been directed at authority figures and has led to violent, assaultive behaviour.

• When turned towards himself, his anger has precipitated ideas of suicide.

• The inappropriate force of his anger and his lack of ability to control or channel it reflect a primary weakness of person-ality structure.

This assessment was endorsed and later expanded upon in a study by the widely respected forensic psychiatrist, Dr Joseph Satten of the Meninger Clinic in Topeka, Kansas. His article 'Murder Without Apparent Motive', published in the *American Journal of Psychiatry* in 1960, outlines his approach. Again it is very useful in our case.

Satten's examination of four convicted murderers in the

category described as 'without motive' is a practice that is continued to this day by profilers in Quantico and elsewhere in the world. His conclusions can be applied to the numerous random and serial killers that followed in US criminal history, and in such murders, both solved and unsolved, in this country.

The characteristics that emerge here include:

• Despite the violence in their lives all the men had ego images of themselves as inferior, weak and inadequate.

• The histories revealed in each a degree of sexual inhibition.

• To all of them adult women were threatening creatures.

• In all four cases there is historical evidence of altered states of consciousness, frequently in connection with the outbursts of violence.

• During moments of actual violence they often felt separated or isolated from themselves, as if they were watching someone else.

• There was a common experience of violence at the hands of family members in their youth.

• Their relationships with others were of a shallow nature and their emotions in relation to the murders and their own fate were also shallow.

• Guilt and remorse were strikingly absent.

• A chance acquaintance, or even a complete stranger was easily able to lose his or her 'real' meaning and assume an identity in the killer's unconscious traumatic configuration.

• When such senseless murders occur, they are seen to be an end result of a period of increasing tension and disorganisation in the murderer, starting before the contact with the victim who, by fitting into the unconscious conflicts of the murderer, unwittingly serves to set in motion his homicidal potential.

* * *

Our profilers agree that the murderer of Sophie Toscan du Plantier is a man who has a deep-seated hatred of women, whom he wishes to punish by torture, violence and murder. They believe he is a sexual deviant with an anal fixation and is into unusual and abnormal sex. Sex and violence have become merged in his mind. According to one profiler, men with such characteristics live for sex/violence in a totally obsessional fashion. Profilers consulted found the following:

• The killer has sexual inadequacies, like premature ejaculation or temporary impotence, which make him obsessive about sex and increase his bitterness and anger towards women.

• He is both attracted to and repelled by strong and successful women. In his fantasies he will make these women do what he wants and, more dangerously, punish them. The rationale is a deviant urge to control, torture, or murder his victim.

• He has an anal fixation and anal sex is a preference that he forces on his sexual partners; the more they protest the more he forces it on them in order to hurt and humiliate them. This is another facet of the deep-seated hatred of women and also suggests a possible repressed homosexual urge.

• He is a risk-taker, and risk is part of the arousal process for him.

* * *

From an early age this type of killer has possessed an extraordinary sex drive and during his formative years this drive was fuelled mainly by fantasy. Psychologists believe that fantasy is the key to the development of sexual perversion. The fantasist feels ashamed of his sexual daydreams and tends to cut himself off from reality, from the outside world, preferring the secret and exciting landscape of his dreams. The dreams are often aided by pornography. Eventually a time will come when the sex dreamer will attempt to translate his fantasies into reality, and he will seek out a situation that brings it all to life. That moment will spell extreme danger for a woman he will want to rape, or even murder.

The infamous American sex serial killer, Ted Bundy, started out as a Peeping Tom as a result of getting an accidental glimpse through a lighted window of a girl undressing. But he graduated to being a stalker and eventually a vicious sex killer, a classic path of progress for this category. By the time he was arrested, four years after his first attack, he was estimated to have been responsible for thirty-four murders. Most men could live with the fantasies derived from seeing a woman undress and leave it at that, without being overwhelmed by the sort of compulsion that drives the sex- or lust-killer to act out his fantasy and in the process destroy not an image but a human being.

The moment when the fantasy is translated into reality can be prompted by a number of different circumstances. Rejection is one of the most common. The effect of sexual advances being rejected can result in instantaneous and savage violence, because the majority of the fantasies are based on the notion of the female as slave to deviant desires. The perpetrator feels only self-pity when he is rejected.

Many such men are childish and undisciplined person-alities, bound by chains of utter selfishness. They usually convey a high opinion of themselves, despite their low self-esteem. The man with such a reaction is not insane. His desire for dominance, subjugation, the infliction of pain and death is the ultimate in the indulgence of his need for power and is a calculated wickedness. Gratification comes from the fear and terror he arouses in his victim.

Power and control are the driving forces. The perpetra-tor does not have these in his own life, but he wants to impose them on someone else in order to boost his self-esteem. This 'control freak' type operates a regime of total obedience at home with his wife or partner, and children. If his instructions are not followed to the letter, he is liable to fly into a rage, both in private and in public. The least sign of opposition is greeted by a completely irrational reaction. There is no debate allowed; he must get his way at all costs. Everything is black and white, and everything this person does, however appalling, is essentially right. This type of person will demand and operate total sexual freedom outside the home, but will throttle his wife or partner if she as much as looks at another man. The urge is one of continual dominance. Inextricably attached to dominance is sex.

Australian sex-killer Ivan Milat showed that such cruelty usually begins at home, where he demanded total obedience. He was obsessive about order and tidiness in the house and when he sent his wife, Karen, shopping with a list, she had to return with every item correct as per the list or he would fly into a rage. When she eventually left him, he burnt down her parents' garage.

Behavioural analysts say that in this 'self-esteem' type of crime the motivation is primarily the desire for recognition – to become known for some achievement, even if that is rape or murder. The crime actually produces a sense of pride and self-worth.

Many such killers revel in the notoriety that their cases bring. One claimed to be the most successful member of his family. Many boast about their crimes in and out of prison.

This type of killer has, the profilers suggest, most likely

depicted his violent sexual fantasies in the form of drawings. These drawings are the most damning evidence of the sick mind of such deviants and they graphically illustrate their fantasies, which are almost always centred around violence towards females and the female body. Breasts, the vagina and the anus are most commonly portrayed as being attacked by instruments such as knives, bottles and hatchets. The penis, when introduced, is depicted as a weapon of torture and punishment.

The representations bestow a power on the illustrator that he cannot match in reality, like the masturbator who becomes impotent when presented with sex. But men who express their desires in this way are unstable and dangerous, because the expression itself does not provide catharsis, it is more in the order of a rehearsal. All that is needed next is the potential victim and the opportunity.

'When that opportunity arises,' explains a forensic psychiatrist, 'nothing apart from a van full of police will stop the killer's urge to fulfil his fantasy, and he will take what most criminals would consider outrageous risks. This is because the normal associations, like being caught, or considering the consequences, are not a factor in the killer's make-up.'

The West Cork killer's motivation when visiting the house of Sophie Toscan du Plantier was probably sex. But when he was rejected he flew into an uncontrollable rage and murder replaced sex. The beating of her face until it was almost unrecognisable is considered an act designed to depersonalise the victim, to rob them of any sense of identity, even in death. It is also, according to profilers, an act of frenzied maiming, which is an equivalent of mutilation of the breasts or genitalia, depriving the victim of her female persona, the characteristic that distinguishes her as a woman. After the murder, the killer derives huge satisfaction from viewing the state of the body. Robbing the victim of their personality is of primary importance.

Another typical characteristic of this type of killer is their ability to implicate other people in their crimes, and convince those people that they too are guilty, equally guilty. Usually, women are the target for this role in the killer's drama, and such people are made to feel intimidated and threatened. One of the most studied relationships in this context is that of Moors murderer Ian Brady and his lover, Myra Hindley.

* * *

Any experienced murder investigator will tell you that it is not easy, given the tremendous advances in technology and DNA testing, to get away with murder nowadays. It is also extremely difficult to dispose of a body successfully. This makes it even more difficult to understand why the case of Sophie Toscan du Plantier, in which the body was found at the site of the murder, has not yet been solved.

Although Sophie's killer disposed of the murder weapon and attempted to wash off some of the gore in a nearby stream (a witness saw a man doing this), his clothes would still have been soaked in blood right through to his undergarments. It would have been very difficult to disguise this. How did he do it? This question remains unanswered.

Another question also arises: having felt what it was like to commit the ultimate brutality – murder – and not get caught, will the killer try again? Experts say that his compulsion will not go away. This makes him highly dangerous because killers who have got away with murder find it easier to repeat the act. According to experts, he is still a danger to others, especially women, and is obsessed with domination and violence. His erratic and violent behaviour will not have stopped through fear of apprehension.

The terrifying thing is that experts in crime and in the criminal mind maintain that it is highly likely that his reign of terror will continue until he kills again.

* * *

Meanwhile, for the grieving husband and family of Sophie Toscan du Plantier and for the people of the West Cork countryside that she so loved, there is no resolution. All that remains are memories ... and hope.

The Libel Hearing

Introduction

Seven years after Sophie Toscan du Plantier's battered body was found in the laneway leading to her holiday home in Toormore, a sensational libel hearing took place in Cork. The action – brought by freelance journalist Ian Bailey against eight Irish and British newspapers – not only revived memories of the murder but introduced into the public domain hitherto unknown details of events both before and after the crime. Ian Bailey sued the newspapers because he claimed that his life, career and reputation had been destroyed through their coverage of the 1996 murder. He alleged that the newspapers had effectively branded him the murderer of Ms Toscan du Plantier, and that as a result he had become 'untouchable' in West Cork. He told the court that he was taking the action not for monetary gain but merely to restore his good name and to prove his innocence of the awful crime.

Ian Bailey was born in Manchester in England in 1957 to middle-class parents. A bright student, he was educated at Gloucester Grammar School. He decided on a career in journalism and in the mid 1970s became a trainee journalist in Gloucester before going to work for a freelance agency there for five years. He then moved to Cheltenham where he operated his own freelance agency – serving a range of broadsheet and tabloid newspapers including the *Times*, the *Daily Mirror*, the *Sunday Times* and the *Daily Telegraph* as well as TV stations including HTV and BBC West. He worked in Cheltenham for eight years – five of which he spent married to a fellow journalist, Sara Limbrick. The marriage ended in separation. Ian Bailey lost interest in journalism in England – deciding that it was 'too frivolous' for him. He eventually resolved to start a new life in Ireland and moved to West Cork in 1991.

After a brief stay in Schull, Bailey moved to Wicklow in a bid to find permanent work. However, he didn't like life in such close proximity to Dublin and returned to Schull in late 1991. He worked for a brief period in the town's fish factory where he first met Welsh-born artist, Jules Thomas, when she came to buy fish. Back home in England he had been interested in gardening; now he turned what had been a hobby into a way of making money, and worked as a gardener for people in the locality. He developed a relationship with Jules Thomas in early 1992 and, after briefly renting accommodation from her, they moved in together in Ms Thomas's home at The Prairie, Liscaha, several miles outside Schull. Bailey's passions soon included Irish culture and, in particular, Irish music. He became a fixture at traditional music sessions around the West Cork area, and learned to play the bodhrán. At such sessions, he would also read samples of his poetry. He began referring to himself as Eoin, rather than Ian, and, on occasion, as Eoin Ó Baille – an Irish-language version of his name.

In late 1995 and early 1996 Bailey took steps to try to revive his journalistic career by making contacts with local media outlets including the *Cork Examiner* (now the *Irish Examiner*) and the *Southern Star*. He also got involved with the West Cork branch of Earthwatch and participated in a FÁS-supported Community Film Project in Skibbereen whose patron was Sir David Puttnam. He had written a script for the project. On 23 December, 1996, when Sophie Toscan du Plantier's body was discovered, the *Cork Examiner*'s West Cork Correspondent, Eddie Cassidy, made contact with the local stringer – Ian Bailey – and asked him to assist in covering the case.

For several days, Ian Bailey supplied Eddie Cassidy with contacts, information and local data about the murder case. His payment for this work was less than €50. However, he also made contact with other media organisations, including the *Irish Star*, the *Sunday Tribune* and *Paris Match* and contributed material to them on the murder.

On 10 February, 1997 Ian Bailey was arrested by Gardaí at the West Cork home he shared with Jules Thomas and taken to Bandon Garda Station for questioning in connection with the murder of Sophie Toscan du Plantier. Jules Thomas was also arrested. After being questioned for almost ten hours they were released without charge. In 1998, Ian Bailey was again arrested and taken to Bandon for questioning. But once again he was released without charge.

Articles published after Bailey's first arrest in 1997 led to him taking libel actions against the *Sunday Independent*, the *Independent on Sunday*, the *Times*, the *Sunday Times*, the *Daily Telegraph*, the *Irish Mirror*, the *Irish Star* and the *Irish Sun*.

THE HEARING

DAY ONE – Monday, 8 December 2003

Ian Bailey arrived at Cork's Camden Quay courthouse shortly after 9.30am. Journalists who had known and interviewed the forty-seven-year-old since he sprang to prominence via the Toscan du Plantier murder investigation in 1996 were taken aback at how aged the former English grammar school boy appeared. Gone was the handsome, raven-haired, dapper man who recited poetry in West Cork pubs and loved to play the bodhrán on Cape Clear. Now,

Ian Bailey appeared older than his years – his hair greying around the temples – as he strode into the courthouse, dressed in a sombre grey tweed suit, and accompanied by his partner, Jules Thomas.

The couple arrived at the courthouse by taxi. Of the two, it was Jules Thomas who betrayed signs of tension. Ian Bailey exuded confidence – as if he had been waiting for this day to arrive for some time. He carried an old leather satchel filled with papers, clippings and notes about the action. For the next two weeks the satchel would remain by his side, acting as a constant source of reference for his own legal team. Studiously ignoring the gathered knot of reporters and photographers, the pair made their way inside the blue-and-white converted garden supplies warehouse that was the temporary home of Cork Circuit Court. A crowd of onlookers had gathered outside the courthouse, curious as to the presence of three TV crews and half-a-dozen photographers. Passing motorists slowed down to see the cause of the flashing cameras.

After conferring with his legal team, Bailey and Thomas entered Courtroom No. 1 – the largest in the court building – shortly before 10am, to await the opening of the proceedings. They sat on the left-hand side of the body of the courtroom, four rows back from the main table that hosted the barristers representing both sides. Such was the media interest in the case that Cork Circuit Court staff had to make special arrangements for the number of reporters and photographers in attendance. The normal press bench – which caters for a maximum of six reporters – was augmented by allocating the entire jury box to the media as well as three rows of seats by the rear wall that would normally be occupied by prisoners and prison officers, and another row along the left-hand wall of the courtroom. As the case opened, the media corps outnumbered the legal teams and the gathered onlookers put together.

Many of those who would later appear as witnesses were already present in the courtroom on day one. Virtually all had been subpoenaed to attend. Others attending were journalists who had covered the case in 1997/1998 and were thought likely to be asked to give evidence about some of the articles complained of. They included Paddy Clancy (*Irish Sun*), Senan Moloney (*Irish Star*), John Kearns (*Irish Mirror*), Eddie Cassidy (*Cork Examiner*) and Deirdre O'Reilly (County Sound FM).

It was a day that many had thought would never arrive. In 2001, when Bailey first signalled his intention to sue for defamation, few believed that the action would ever see the inside of a courtroom. Fewer still would have expected the action, if it did proceed, to be heard in the Circuit Court rather than the High Court. The maximum damages that can be awarded per case by the Circuit Court is €38,000 so, even if Ian Bailey won all seven of his actions, the total amount he stood to receive would not exceed €266,000 – hardly a significant sum of money given the nature of the defamation complaints he had made. (Although eight newspapers were being sued, there were seven actions listed, because the *Times* and its sister title, the *Sunday Times*, were listed as a single action.) Had Bailey taken the action in the High Court and won, the damages could, in theory, be limitless. However, a key difference between a defamation action taken in the Circuit Court as against the High Court is that, in the former, the case is heard before a judge only, while in the High Court the action is decided by a judge and jury.

Representing Ian Bailey were Bandon-based solicitor Con Murphy and barrister Jim Duggan. Murphy had acted for Ian Bailey since 1996 and represented him on both the occasions on which he was arrested in connection with the investigation into Sophie Toscan du Plantier's death. It was against Murphy's advice that, in the wake of his first arrest, Ian Bailey agreed to a number of radio and newspaper interviews. Jim Duggan BL ranked as one of the leading members of the bar in Cork, and was a veteran of both civil and criminal matters.

The eight newspapers had assembled a high-powered defence team. Instructed by four separate firms of solicitors, the team was led by Paul Gallagher SC and included David Holland SC. The opening session of the hearing was dominated by legal submissions, the results of which, though it was not realised at the time, would have a crucial bearing on the proceedings and on the outcome of the case. It quickly became apparent that the newspapers were committed to a full, far-reaching and vigorous defence of their action. They demanded access to key elements of the State's file on the Toscan du Plantier case – including Ian Bailey's own diaries – which were taken and retained by the Gardaí after his arrests in 1997/98.

The State, which was not a party to the defamation action, objected to the calling of any Gardaí involved in the murder investigation as witnesses in the libel action. The State also raised objections to any of the material it had compiled as part of that investigation being used in a civil proceeding. Their concern was rooted in the fear that such access to witnesses and information could ultimately jeopardise any action that the Director of Public Prosecutions might sanction in relation to the murder.

Paul Gallagher, on behalf of the newspapers, cited ample case law to support the case for disclosure of the material. He also referred to a letter from the Director of Public Prosecutions, which was read into the court record. That letter, dated March 2003, confirmed that while the DPP viewed the murder file on Sophie Toscan du Plantier's killing as open, there were no plans for a prosecution. Judge Patrick J Moran then granted an order allowing the defence access to

Sophie on a trip to India.

Above: Sophie in contemplative mood at Daniel's country house in Ambax.
Below: Sophie on a boating holiday in Sicily.

Above: The house in West Cork that Sophie had chosen as a refuge and retreat from her hectic life in France.
Below: A relaxed summer lunch outside the house in Toormore.

Above: Sophie's parents Georges and Marguerite by the turf fire in Toormore in October 1996, just months before their daughter's murder. *Below:* A view from the house, showing the landscape that Sophie loved.

Above: Marguerite,
Marie Madeleine and Georges
return to Toormore,
summer 2002.

Left: Sophie's parents look out
across the valley towards
Dunmanus Bay.

A Celtic cross with the simple inscription 'Sophie'
stands on the spot where she was murdered.

Above: Cavity blocks beside the laneway in Toormore. A similar block found close to the body is thought to be one of the murder weapons.
Below: Sophie's final resting place is a flower-strewn grave in the small cemetery at Ambax, near Toulouse.

Above: Sophie's parents beside the traditional open fireplace
in the livingroom in Dunmanus West.
Below: Sophie's charm and beauty endeared her to all who met her.

the materials they required. This ruling meant that Ian Bailey's own diaries and intimate writings could now be used against him, but no one in the courtroom that day could have realised just how explosive that material would be.

The hearing proper began shortly after twelve noon when Ian Bailey's counsel, Jim Duggan BL, set out his client's case against the eight newspapers. In classic jurist pose, Mr Duggan painted a picture of how Ian Bailey's life and reputation had been affected by the actions of the newspapers cited, pointing out that 'these monstrous articles' had left the English journalist in a 'living nightmare'. 'These slanted and biased pieces have resulted in Ian Bailey being shunned by society,' Jim Duggan asserted. 'Within his own community he is referred to as "the murderer". He has been persecuted and victimised. He has been living a horror story. But he lives with just one hope – a hope that some day someone may be tried for this horrific crime.'

The case was Ian Bailey's attempt to clear his good name, Mr Duggan declared. 'Ian Bailey did not bring this case lightly. If it were for purely financial purposes he would not have brought [the actions] in this jurisdiction ... He has brought this case in the hope he might find some method of showing ordinary people that he is not the murderer and that he did not kill Sophie Toscan du Plantier.'

'I don't know whether Ian Bailey committed this murder or not,' Jim Duggan said. 'He says he did not and I accept it.

But this was not enough for the Fourth Estate [the media]. They decided he was guilty and there has been trial by media, character assassination and demonisation.' The barrister went on to say that his client 'remains persecuted and victimised. He has been DNAed; his hair, his blood and his clothes. Nothing. No charges have ever been brought.'

His client was not in court to try and persuade anyone that he was 'a saint', Jim Duggan added. But such was the grossly defamatory nature of the articles published by the eight newspapers that he had no other option but to resort to the law to prove his innocence of the slurs involved.

Paul Gallagher, for the newspapers, said that the defence would contend that Ian Bailey was the main and only suspect for the murder when the newspaper articles were published. They would claim that Mr Bailey was and is 'a very violent man', and that he himself had courted publicity about the du Plantier murder.

The hearing was adjourned for lunch, and when it resumed at 2.15pm, Jim Duggan began a detailed litany of the articles complained of, describing them as salacious, defamatory and hurtful. He showed the court some of the headlines that had appeared after his client had been identified in print as a suspect in the murder: 'Investigating With the Prime Suspect' in the *Sunday Independent*, 'A Devil In the Hills' in the *Independent on Sunday*, 'Bailey In £500,000 Divorce Row' in the *Irish Star* and 'Sophie Man's Shame' in the *Irish Sun*. A piece in the *Daily Telegraph* said that the suspect in the French woman's murder had been working on a film script; an *Irish Mirror* article said that the suspect in Sophie Toscan du Plantier's murder had a history of violence against women.

For over an hour, the barrister went through the newspaper reports, citing allegation after allegation that he claimed had distorted and destroyed his client's good reputation. And, he emphasised, these articles were merely the very worst of those that had tainted Ian Bailey's reputation; he maintained that if he were to list all the articles that had defamed his client, the hearing could last for months.

Throughout the lengthy opening, Ian Bailey remained calm and impassive in the body of the courtroom, with Jules Thomas by his side. At 3.35pm, having finished his outline of the complaint, Jim Duggan turned and asked Ian Bailey to take the stand. The English journalist stood, smoothed down his jacket and exchanged a few brief words with Jules Thomas. As he proceeded to the stand, he looked composed and assured, showing all the signs of a man convinced that the law was on his side.

Ian Bailey's Evidence

Ian Bailey accepted the New Testament from the court registrar. In a clipped, quiet but determined voice, he vowed to tell the truth, pausing as he made the promise as if to emphasise the point. Then, in reply to a series of questions from his barrister, Bailey outlined his background, why he came to Ireland and how he first met Jules Thomas.

'I met her when she came to the Schull [fish] factory looking for some fish,' he explained. 'We kept meeting each other [in Schull] ... I was looking for a place to live and she had another home. But as time went by we became closer and closer.' After a time living together, Ian Bailey found himself helping Jules Thomas with the raising of her three daughters. 'I worked there ... I did quite a lot. Anything that I could help with. Jules Thomas was off the road at the time with a driving ban so I collected the girls [from school]. I spent a good bit of time helping her with the parenting. We fell in love.'

Jim Duggan asked Ian Bailey when he had decided to revive his journalistic career in West Cork. 'I had never really stopped working as a journalist,' he explained. 'I had supplied stories on an occasional basis [to the *Cork Examiner/Southern Star*].' He continued to get gardening and maintenance work. But he eventually decided to get more involved in journalism and took time to introduce himself to the various news reporters and editors in Cork.

Jim Duggan then began a detailed series of questions on how Ian Bailey got involved in covering the Sophie Toscan du Plantier murder story on 23 December 1996 and what he had been doing on the morning of the murder.

Bailey was adamant that the only time he had seen Sophie Toscan du Plantier was some eighteen months before her death, when she was pointed out to him, several hundred metres away, through the window of a neighbour's house. The only reason he went to the murder scene on 23 December was at the request of the *Cork Examiner*.

'I received a phone call from Eddie Cassidy [*Cork Examiner*] shortly before lunch,' Bailey explained. 'I was asked if I could maybe find out about the incident. He said there had been a murder and that it involved a foreign national. It was thought the person may have been French.' Bailey insisted that this phone call was the first he had heard of the murder.

Ian Bailey said that before he got the phone call, he had been preparing turkeys for Christmas Day. 'We used to rear free-range turkeys. The idea was to sell one and cover the cost of the other one, which we would eat. We were fairly self-sufficient.' As it was only two days before Christmas, he had been getting the turkeys ready, both for their own Christmas dinner and for market. Jim Duggan asked him to say precisely what he had been doing. 'The turkeys were being prepared for the table. I had to kill them. But I got one small scratch from a talon as I did the job. I used a knife. But it's not a job I enjoy. And we just don't do it anymore.'

He had also been sourcing the family's Christmas tree. Accompanied by Saffron, Jules' daughter, he picked out a tall fir tree that was growing locally. 'It was twenty feet high or so. I had to scale it and cut the top off it. It was a very difficult job. And I did get some scratches on my arms,' he explained to Jim Duggan. (It had been reported by people who met Ian Bailey on the day of the murder that he had scratches on his arms and face.)

When he received the phone call from Eddie Cassidy he immediately agreed to see if he could find out what was happening at Toormore, the area where it had been reported that a body was found. 'I went to the lane and I could see Gardaí and a lot of activity on the hillside. A little later, a few Gardaí came up to me and I explained that I was there for the *Cork Examiner*. They told me to contact the Garda press office.'

After they had moved some distance from the scene, Jules Thomas, who had accompanied Bailey, took some photos, using a long lens camera.

The couple then decided to go to the local post office to try and find out more about what had occurred. 'The word was spreading that a terrible thing had happened. I was trying to find out about a name.' When asked by Jim Duggan what he found out, Ian Bailey said that he eventually discovered the name of the victim. 'In fact, I thought I had got the name wrong, but it turned out to be [her] maiden name.' Sophie Toscan du Plantier was known locally by her maiden name of Bouniol.

Bailey filed copy on the murder for both the *Cork*

Examiner and the *Irish Independent* but the pieces were not published. He told the Court that he ultimately ended up working on the story for the *Sunday Tribune*, the *Irish Star* and a French magazine, *Paris Match*.

Shortly before 5 pm, Judge Moran adjourned the hearing for the day. The complex legal submissions had taken up so much of the first day that very little progress had been made. Observers and members of the media feared that they were in for a very long haul. Few could have guessed at the sensational turn of events that would shortly tranform the hearing into a national fixation.

DAY TWO – Tuesday, 9 December

The second day of the hearing opened with Ian Bailey once again in the stand. His barrister asked him about his arrest on 10 February 1997 at the Liscaha house he shared with Jules Thomas. Bailey declared himself 'flabbergasted, shocked and surprised' to be arrested. He claimed that he initially received a friendly reception from the Gardaí, but that once he was handcuffed and placed inside the squad car outside his home he found the atmosphere dramatically different. He claimed that Gardaí had tried to frighten him into admitting the murder.

'Shortly after we were on the road the atmosphere towards me changed to what I can only describe as one of great hostility. I was bombarded with verbal claims and allegations.' He was convinced that his treatment at the hands of the Gardaí had been part of an 'orchestrated and premeditated routine'. Bailey claimed that at one point a Garda warned him that they had 'cast-iron evidence' that would 'put me away for life'. Another Garda said to him: 'even if we can't pin this on you ...,' [I] 'was finished in Ireland'. He alleged that he was told: 'You could be found dead with a bullet in the back of the head.'

Bailey said the Gardaí took a roundabout route to Bandon Garda Station and when they arrived, they found the station mobbed by reporters and photographers. 'There was a mêlée ... a mayhem of media,' he claimed. He described to his counsel how, in a frantic bid to protect his identity, he extended the headrest in the squad car to try and shield his face. However, the Gardaí left the station gate open and one photographer got in, snatching a photo of Bailey as he was led, in handcuffs, into the station. Once inside, he claimed that he was subjected to a ferocious round of questioning, during which he was warned by Gardaí that there was 'a hanging mob' outside the station for him. 'They told me that everybody accepted that I was the killer and they said there was cast-iron evidence that Jules reluctantly accepted that I was the killer. They told me to come clean and clear my conscience', he added. He was stripped, and blood and hair samples were taken for DNA testing. 'I knew I had nothing to hide. So I had no fears about giving blood or DNA,' he said.

The day after the arrest, 11 February, Ian Bailey's name first appeared in print – in the *Irish Sun* – as a suspect in the murder case, accompanied by a photograph of him. He became the target of the national and international media. When asked by Jim Duggan how he felt about the coverage he had received, Ian Bailey paused, briefly closed his eyes, and said that he was shocked at how he was portrayed. He 'felt sick to the pit of [his] stomach' after reading one article – following an interview he had only given because the reporter had promised a sympathetic piece. The impact of the newspaper articles on his life in West Cork was utterly devastating. 'I am still to some degree untouchable,' Ian Bailey asserted. 'I was stripped of my presumption of innocence. I used to go out when I wanted to. I'd go to Bantry or Skibbereen. I don't do that anymore. Life has been a struggle. It feels like I am being eaten alive. I have been battered [by the media].'

In January 1998 Ian Bailey was again arrested in connection with the murder, but was released without charge. He told Jim Duggan that the trauma of the two arrests induced a 'flight or fight feeling' in him. But he never left West Cork because he felt the allegation had to be challenged and his innocence proven. 'It didn't even occur to me [to leave Ireland]. Wherever one would go in this world, this would follow. And there was no question of running away from this. But there were times when I felt like a hunted animal.'

Jim Duggan then slowly and carefully took Ian Bailey through each of the articles complained of in the eight newspapers. The cumulative effect of that coverage, Ian Bailey said, was to make him feel as if a campaign was being waged against him.

Aware that the defendants would undoubtedly raise the matter of Ian Bailey's arrests in 1996 and 2001 for violent incidents against Jules Thomas, Jim Duggan asked his client to talk about these events.

'It is to my eternal regret that during our thirteen years together we have had three fights,' Ian Bailey responded. 'But I accept full responsibility for what happened. I hurt her and I admitted it.' He said that he had been 'under a lot of pressure from external forces' when the incident in 2001 occurred. At that point 'we had been under the most extraordinary pressure for five years. But I am not going to defend what I did. Over a period of time, we made it up. But I am not proud of what happened.'

Shortly after 3 pm, Ian Bailey finished answering questions from his barrister. As Jim Duggan sat down, Paul Gallagher SC, lead counsel for the defendants, stepped up to begin his cross-examination. Ian Bailey slowly sipped water as the senior counsel immediately challenged him on his version of the assaults on Jules Thomas. He put it to Mr Bailey that he was trying to play down the seriousness of the

assaults, one of which Bailey had described as 'an indiscretion'. Referring to the attack on Ms Thomas in 1996 as the
couple were returning from a party, he pointed out that her
injuries included bite marks, a mouth wound requiring
eight stitches, a badly bruised eye and that clumps of hair
had been torn from her scalp.

'How would you describe the person who did that?' Mr
Gallagher asked.

'Not very nice,' Ian Bailey replied, adding, 'It is appalling.'

Mr Gallagher asked whether 'appalling' was as far as he
was prepared to go. 'Would you think it was animal-like?'

'No' Ian Bailey replied.

He denied that he had torn out clumps of Ms Thomas's
hair and said that they had come out because she had a scalp
condition. He went on to insist that he was not prone to
violence.

'I am not a violent man. This was not a premeditated att-
tack. All the violence between us occurred with drink. I
didn't intend to hurt her,' he said. He said that Ms Thomas
had started the incident. 'If she had not started to go at my
face this would not have happened. I am not a violent
person. When we both drink, violence occurs. I believe
there is a difference.'

DAY THREE – Wednesday, 10 December
Paul Gallagher returned to his examination of the facts

relating to the assaults on Jules Thomas. He referred to the incident in 2001 when Ian Bailey had struck his partner with a crutch. 'It was something that happened very quickly – in a flash,' Bailey said.

Despite agreeing with the descriptions in witness statements as to the extent of Ms Thomas's injuries, and under pressure from Mr Gallagher to 'tell the whole truth', Bailey continued to maintain that he was not a violent man.

Paul Gallagher then produced extracts from Ian Bailey's own diaries, and there followed a series of quotations that stunned the crowd in the packed courtroom. Journalists quickly revised their projected copy for the day as the significance of what they were hearing became apparent. Now the newspaper's insistence from day one on getting access to the diaries made sense. These were very potent weapons. While Ian Bailey denied that he was violent, his own diaries painted a very different picture.

Paul Gallagher read aloud from an entry made by Bailey in 1993: 'I never had a history of violence towards women, yet of late … I have on a number of occasions struck and abused my lover.'

In 1996, Bailey wrote: 'One act of whiskey-induced madness, coupled and cracked, and in an act of awful violence I severely damaged you and made you feel that death was near. As I lay and write, I know there is something badly wrong with me. For through remorse-filled sentiments,

disgust fills me. I am afraid for myself – a cowardly fear …
For although I have damaged and made grief your life, I
have damaged my own destiny and future to the point
where I am seeing, in destroying you, I destroyed me.' 'But
in doing what I did, I am damned to hell,' the diary added.

On 15 May 1996, just two weeks after the attack on
Jules Thomas, he recorded:

'I actually tried to kill her. I feel a sense of sickness at
seeing my own account of the attack that night … I am an
animal on two feet.'

Paul Gallagher questioned Bailey about each of the diary
statements, asking him what they meant, what he had been
trying to say.

All these references, the plaintiff argued, were written 'in
an abstract form' and should not be taken literally. He told
the court that if the extracts were read out to him he would
think they were the work of a poet such as Dylan Thomas.
'A lot of what I write is imagination. It's the way I approach
my creative writing. I grew up with Dylan Thomas,' Ian
Bailey said, explaining that the Welsh poet also regularly
referred to death in his writings.

This literary allusion made little impression on Paul Gallagher who again and again contrasted Mr Bailey's diary
writings with his vague opening description to the court
about the nature of the domestic violence to which he had
subjected Jules Thomas. Paul Gallagher challenged Ian

Bailey as to how he could downplay a fight with his partner on 1 May 1996 as 'an indiscretion' – and not elaborate on 'the horrific violence involved'. The full details of the attack were 'very significant' as gleaned from the diary.

The court heard that when they arrived home that night, Ian Bailey was hysterical and refused to hand over keys to Ms Thomas's daughter, Virginia, so that her mother could be taken to hospital. She ultimately had to be taken for medical treatment by a neighbour, Peter Bielecki. For the next three weeks, Mr Bielecki looked after Ms Thomas's children in her home while the artist was receiving treatment in a Cork hospital.

Bailey also accepted after repeated questioning that he had probably hit Ms Thomas in Cork city in 1993, after which she required hospital treatment.

In August 2001, the third and last of the assaults, he claimed he had only struck Jules Thomas with his plaster-encased leg and a crutch because he was in pain from an injury and feeling the effects of alcohol on strong medication. The matter later resulted in a District Court prosecution – with Ian Bailey being fined and given a three-month suspended sentence after he pleaded guilty to the assault. As he was unable to come up with bail, he spent a number of weeks on remand in Cork Prison.

He claimed that the Gardaí, and some people in West Cork who didn't like him, viewed as 'a little gift from heaven into their lap' his arrest in August 2001. Taken into custody at Cork airport as he was about to take a flight to England, he insisted he was only going away to 'give Jules and the lads some breathing space'.

'There is no justification for domestic violence. It is far too prevalent in this country,' he told the court. 'But the fact that I have committed these with Jules doesn't mean that I am a murderer.'

The court heard that a number of witnesses would testify that Ian Bailey had confessed to killing Sophie Toscan du Plantier. Paul Gallagher said that the Shellys, a couple who had been invited to Liscaha on New Year's Eve in 1998, were confronted by a sobbing Bailey, who said, 'I did it, I did it, I went too far.' He also claimed that Bailey had confessed to the news editor of the *Sunday Tribune*, as well as to Bill Fuller, Yvonne Ungerer and schoolboy Malachi Reed. Ian Bailey refuted these suggestions, saying that he was only repeating rumours that he was the murderer. 'I only said that it was being said that I was the murderer,' he claimed.

Ian Bailey's evidence was then interruped to allow short testimony from Colman Doyle, a veteran journalist who worked on the Sophie Toscan du Plantier murder story. He told the hearing he was shocked at how Ian Bailey was depicted in the media after his first arrest. 'I thought he was being demonised,' explained Mr Doyle, who said he found Ian Bailey 'an excellent journalist and a nice person.'

DAY FOUR – Thursday, 11 December

As Ian Bailey began the fourth day of evidence, the pressure on him was all too evident. He told Judge Patrick Moran that he was feeling the strain; he was finding it difficult to sleep and was extremely tired. Since the diary revelations the trial had become a huge public attraction. Pensioners, shoppers, and even barristers would queue to grab a vacant seat in the packed courtroom. Such was the interest that Cork radio stations Red FM and County Sound/96 FM carried hourly updates on the case.

At times, Ian Bailey reacted with incredulity to Paul Gallagher as he outlined the allegations that would be levelled against him by independent West Cork witnesses. At one point, threatening to lose the calm that marked his demeanour throughout the hearing, he vehemently protested that he was the victim of 'lies, fabrications and untruths'. But, as the Senior Counsel directly put witness claim after witness claim to Ian Bailey, the whole atmosphere of the hearing palpably changed.

Ian Bailey's barrister, Jim Duggan, protested at the direction the defence was taking and asked how far the defence was going to go in defending the defamation case. He said it had never been claimed by the defence that they would say that Ian Bailey committed the crime.

Judge Moran cautioned Paul Gallagher that he was 'taking on the mantle of a prosecution case and cross-examining the plaintiff as if he were the accused. He is not an accused.'

'We have to be careful that this court does not become an inquiry into the murder of Ms du Plantier,' the judge added, pointing out that nobody has been charged with the murder.

Despite the judge's warning, Ian Bailey found himself faced with direct claims that he had admitted killing Sophie Toscan du Plantier. He also heard that it would be said that he had been introduced to the French woman, that he was near her home on the night she was killed and that he had threatened one Schull shopkeeper in a bid to suppress evidence that might incriminate him.

He insisted to the court that he was merely repeating local rumours about the murder in West Cork. Such rumour repetitions did not, he said, represent an admission that he committed the murder. In one case, Mr Bailey denied having said to local man, Bill Fuller, speaking in the second person: 'Yes, you did it, didn't you. You saw her [Sophie] in Spar and she turned you on walking up the aisle with her tight arse ...' 'You went there [Toormore] to see what you could get but she wasn't interested. You chased her and then stirred something in the back of your head and then you went a lot further than you intended to.'

But he did admit that, when it was put to him by *Sunday Tribune* news editor, Helen Callanan, that it was being suggested he was the murderer, he replied 'Oh yes'. 'People were asking her who Eoin Bailey was. At one point she said that it was being said that I was the killer. I said "Yes, that's right". I said it in jest,' he told the court. 'She said to me that it was being said that I was the murderer. I jokingly responded "Oh yes". I wasn't laughing but I didn't take the allegation seriously – it was said in a lighthearted way. How did she take it – did she take it seriously? It was banter – I heard it from some other journalist that I was supposed to have done it but I really wasn't taking it seriously,' Mr Bailey added.

Bailey also admitted telling a local woman, Yvonne Ungerer, that he had killed Ms du Plantier and used a concrete block. 'But I was just reiterating my conversation with Ms Callanan to Ms Ungerer. I was not in anyway serious and I don't think she took it seriously,' the plaintiff explained.

In the case of Ritchie and Rosie Shelly, he admitted he could understand how they became convinced that he was the killer. A New Year's Eve party at his home in 1998, which was attended by the couple, was allegedly dominated by Bailey showing off his scrapbook on the Sophie Toscan du Plantier murder. The Shellys intended to stay overnight but changed their minds, and as they were leaving, they claimed that Bailey came into the hall and said: 'I did it, I did it – I went too far'. But now he insisted that he was merely repeating what he called 'a mantra' that was repeatedly put to him by two Garda detectives during his interrogation.

When the hearing resumed after lunch, Paul Gallagher put it to Ian Bailey that a fourteen-year old schoolboy, Malachi Reed, would also claim that Bailey had admitted the murder to him. Mr Bailey said he offered the youth a lift and merely repeated rumours that were circulating about him and the death of Sophie Toscan du Plantier. 'It was a topic of conversation,' he claimed. He denied that he had said he bashed the Frenchwoman's head in with a rock.

He also flatly rejected suggestions that he could have told three local people on the morning of 23 December that a murder/big story had taken place. 'I can't have done. They have got their times wrong,' Mr. Bailey declared, insisting that he had not learned about the killing until lunchtime when he received a phone call from journalist Eddie Cassidy.

When Paul Gallagher put it to him that he had actually been courting publicity over the crime and his subsequent arrest, Ian Bailey rejected the suggestion, despite the fact that he had agreed to do an RTÉ TV interview immediately after his arrest and subsequently a detailed RTÉ radio interview with Pat Kenny. In that interview – and before the publication of all bar one of the allegedly defamatory newspaper articles – Mr Bailey had said that it was 'quite reasonable' for him to be regarded as a suspect given that he had scratches on his hands.

DAY FIVE – Friday, 12 December

For his fifth and final day of evidence Ian Bailey arrived in court wearing a blue blazer – changing his court routine for the first and only time during the hearing. The day opened in bizarre fashion amid allegations of intimidation and a mysterious Garda operation that Ian Bailey claimed was targeting him.

Bailey formally complained to Judge Patrick Moran that he felt two witnesses – Bill Fuller and Peter Bielecki – were trying to intimidate him. Mr Bailey claimed that Bill Fuller, on meeting the plaintiff in the hallway of the courthouse, had passed the comment: 'I've got you now'. He also alleged that another witness, Peter Bielecki, had been glaring across the courtroom at him 'in a most intense fashion'.

Judge Moran said that, while he was not making any judgement on the accuracy or inaccuracy of Mr Bailey's claims, he could not tolerate any suggestion of intimidation in or near his court. Stressing that his direction should not in any way reflect on the good names of both witnesses, he directed that Bill Fuller and Bielecki be excluded until it was time for them to give evidence.

Then, Ian Bailey claimed that a Garda operation was underway near where he was staying in Cork city for the duration of the court case. 'Something very, very strange is going on,' he declared. He maintained that his papers had been moved and interfered with – and he was certain a Garda operation was in progress which was not in accordance with the law.

Looking tired and frustrated, Bailey launched a scathing attack on West Cork Gardaí, even claiming that a senior Garda had told him that, on the night of the murder, he must have acted like 'a werewolf monster' because there was 'a kind of full moon'. 'We have evidence to show that there were efforts to pervert the course of justice,' he told the court. Judge Moran immediately interjected and warned Mr Bailey that this was a defamation action and nothing more.

Throughout the hearing, Mr Bailey claimed that his efforts to prove the defamation case were hampered by the refusal of Gardaí to release key documentation, including his diaries, which were seized as part of the murder investigation. He acknowledged that, in another swipe at Gardaí, he had told journalists that the Gardaí were trying to 'stitch me up' for the murder of Sophie Toscan du Plantier. 'I still believe that if they could, they would,' he asserted. 'I have been highly critical of them [the Gardaí] right from the beginning,' Mr Bailey added. He said that at one point he was receiving almost daily visits from the Gardaí.

The cross-examination then concluded and Ian Bailey left the witness box. As he resumed his seat in the courtroom beside Jules Thomas, she briefly squeezed his hand and they

exchanged a few words. It had been a marathon and gruelling interrogation, which had lasted the best part of four full
days. As Judge Moran was later to remark, Ian Bailey never
once lost his cool during five days of intense evidence and
cross-examination. The only time he appeared aggrieved
was when it was put to him that an unnamed West Cork
fisherman had complained that he was 'a bad poet and a
brutal bodhrán player'. Mr Bailey responded that his per-
formance had been greeted with enthusiastic applause
during a festival on Cape Clear.

* * *

Jim Duggan then called on Mr Bailey's solicitor, Con
Murphy, Jules Thomas's mother, Beryl-Ann, and Ms Thomas's eldest daughter, Saffron (29), to give evidence.

Mr Murphy's evidence focused on a claim from Marie
Farrell – a West Cork shopkeeper due to give evidence later
– that Ian Bailey had tried to intimidate her. Mrs Farrell had
got a solicitor, Rachel O'Toole, to write to Ian Bailey asking
him to desist. The letter was sent to Con Murphy, who consulted with his client on the matter. 'He [Ian Bailey] denied
it totally,' Mr Murphy told the court. However, Mr
Murphy advised Mr Bailey that, in light of Marie Farrell's
claims, under no circumstances was he to go near her. The
Bandon solicitor also described to the court how 'hordes of
journalists' descended on the town after Ian Bailey's arrests

in 1997 and 1998. 'There were dozens of them. There was a horde of newspaper men and photographers around Bandon Garda Station,' he explained, pointing out that, at one point, a photographer had scaled a six foot high wall behind his Bandon office in an attempt to get a shot of Ian Bailey.

Beryl-Ann Thomas, mother of Jules Thomas, offered brief evidence about Ian Bailey. Ms Thomas – also an artist, known for what she termed her 'nudes' – described Ian Bailey as 'fine – a normal human being'. In reference to the details of the domestic violence incidents to which Ian Bailey had subjected her daughter, Ms Thomas said, 'The past is the past – the future is the only thing. All men are aggressive, aren't they? Let women rule the world.'

Her evidence was followed by the testimony of her granddaughter, Saffron, who gave an emotional account of the effect on the family of the coverage of the Sophie Toscan du Plantier murder. Saffron, the eldest of Jules Thomas's three children, described the coverage as 'disgusting. I was sick to my stomach. I just couldn't believe it. It was just that my family was implicated in the matter,' she explained. Ms Thomas broke down while trying to explain to the court how both Ian Bailey and her mother were devastated by the media coverage. 'They cried every day, my Lord, for about two years. People [in West Cork] didn't know whether to talk to them or not,' she added. 'It's like a big, heavy weight on us all. It's like a dark cloud that just never goes away.'

Shortly after 3.30pm, Jules Thomas took the witness box. She began her evidence by telling how she came to Ireland and detailing her relationship with Ian Bailey, describing their family life together. The Welsh-born artist told the court that she had moved to Ireland in 1973 and had been based in West Cork ever since. She painted extensively and said that she was best known for her landscapes and wildlife work. Her pieces had been featured in heritage centres in such places as Lough Neagh, Killaloe and Mizen Head. She confirmed that she had met Ian Bailey while trying to purchase fish from the Schull factory. After getting to know the freelance journalist and realising that he was looking for a place to stay, she mentioned her studio house, which, because of its spartan condition, was difficult to rent out. But, after agreeing to move in, Ian Bailey became 'the man about the house'. He helped with maintenance, gardening tasks and with raising the children. 'He was always very helpful with the [children's] homework. It was just a normal, family life,' she told Jim Duggan.

Jim Duggan asked her about the assaults by Ian Bailey. Ms Thomas said that the first incident occurred in Cork city when they were sharing a small bed in a friend's house. She described it as 'a tussle more than a fight. It was a moment of alcoholic madness.' Of the second assault, in the car in 1996, she said that it too was provoked by drink-fuelled temper and was over in moments. In time, Ms Thomas added, she had forgiven her partner and knew that he was very sorry for what he did.

Paul Gallagher then began his cross-examination of Ms Thomas, and immediately focused on the assaults she had suffered at the hands of her partner. However, Ms Thomas had just time to reiterate her description of the incidents as 'a tussle' and that they were over in a matter of minutes, before it was decided to adjourn the case for the weekend. The questioning would recommence on Monday morning.

DAY SIX – Monday, 15 December

The second week of the trial opened with statements from two character witnesses: Skibbereen newsagent Brendan Houlihan, and a Schull businessman, Thomas Brosnan. Both said they noticed a dramatic change in Ian Bailey once the media had reported on him as the suspect in the murder probe. Mr Houlihan said that 'a kind of hush-hush' would come from customers in his shop after Mr Bailey would walk in. 'He was branded. He was branded as the murderer,' Mr Houlihan declared. Mr Brosnan remarked that 'If you believed what you read in the papers you would more or less say he was convicted.'

When Jules Thomas re-entered the witness box to resume her evidence, she gave a staunch defence of her partner, and a bitter appraisal of how the media had behaved towards the couple. She claimed the media had been 'sabotaging' their lives through the coverage of the Sophie Toscan du Plantier murder investigation and the fact that Ian Bailey remains the prime Garda suspect.

'Those seven years of pain and suffering ... have been a million times worse than any beatings,' she told a hushed courtroom. Ms Thomas claimed that she still suffers from nightmares, cannot form a regular sleep pattern, has seen friends and neighbours shy away from herself and Ian Bailey and has even found it hard to continue with her painting. 'The overall feeling is that our lives have been sabotaged. I don't feel like a free citizen, actually. Some people actually crossed the road so as not to make contact with us. It was just so, so uggh! He [Ian] was someone that somebody just couldn't go near. It's all part and parcel of being massively harrassed all the time. Detectives even told our friends that Ian was guilty. The articles were sensationalistic and inaccurate. We were deeply upset by it all.'

She first realised the likely extent of the media interest on 10 February 1997 when both she and Ian Bailey were arrested. Ms Thomas told Cork Circuit Civil Court that she had asked for a coat to cover her head in the Garda squad car on the way to Bandon. When, after twelve hours of questioning, she was released without charge and went home, she claimed she was met by an incredible sight.

'The press were absolutely unbelievable. We were

actually under siege [at their Schull home]. It was completely over the top. We were just stunned by it all,' she stated. She said that, at one stage, her youngest daughter, Funella, had to take a week off school and sit, peering out the window, to spot any press that trespassed onto their property. 'We had no light in our house for six weeks because we had to keep all the curtains drawn,' she explained. 'Our lives were completely and utterly disrupted. It would be very hard for anyone to put themselves in our position at the time and imagine what it was all like.'

Under questioning by David Holland SC for the newspapers, Ms Thomas flatly denied several of the key witness allegations levelled against her partner. She said that Ian Bailey had never admitted to the murder and that one witness, Marie Farrell, had approached them herself about an alleged Garda conspiracy. The Welsh artist also complained about her treatment at the hands of the Gardaí who, she claimed, put her and other local people 'under enormous pressure' to make statements. She disputed key elements of the first statement taken from her by Gardaí in February 1997, saying she could not recall having said them. In relation to apparent discrepancies between her 1997 account of the night of 22 December 1996 and subsequent accounts, she insisted that things she never uttered were included. She denied that she had ever told Gardaí that Bailey had a 'raw, fresh and big bloody' cut on his forehead the morning after

Sophie Toscan du Plantier was killed.

'They didn't seem to want to believe what I was saying. They kept putting words in my mouth,' Ms Thomas declared. She told Judge Patrick Moran that she was 'very unhappy' with details contained in the original statement of her interview with Gardaí. She was so concerned that she instructed a solicitor to write to Gardaí advising that she was not accepting several items in the statement – despite having signed it as accurate on leaving the station and subsequently signing a second memo that her statement was accurate. Ms Thomas said that she was convinced Ian Bailey had stayed up in her kitchen writing throughout the early hours of 23 December 1996. But she had no idea what time he got up – or what time he may have come back to bed. 'He was not tossing and turning like it says [in the statement]. We curled up together, absolutely still. But I have no knowledge of what time he may have got up. I was not conscious,' Ms Thomas declared. 'I vaguely remember him getting back into bed,' she added, denying Garda suggestions that Mr Bailey was cold, as if he had been outside the house. She told the court that, on getting up that morning, she found a large handwritten article by Ian Bailey on the table, indicating he had worked a lot that night.

Ms Thomas also denied as inaccurate quotes from her original Garda statement that she felt 'duped' by Ian Bailey, and that, after some witness claims were put to her about her partner that she could have replied, 'maybe I am believing it'.

And she insisted that Ritchie and Rosie Shelly had confused what Ian Bailey was saying to them on New Year's Eve 1998. She was 'very surprised' when the couple decided to leave early, but she understood that Ian Bailey was not making an admission to them about the crime; he was merely repeating what Gardaí had said to him.

In reference to the domestic violence to which Ian Bailey subjected her, Ms Thomas told David Holland she trusted her partner that it would never happen again. 'Alcohol is a strange thing … but he does not drink at all now,' she declared. She denied that Ian Bailey had ever tried to kill her – despite having written in his own diary that he did. 'I believe that when he writes, he exaggerates the situation,' she claimed. When queried about why Mr Bailey should write that he tried to kill her she replied, 'But he hadn't killed me. Nothing like it.'

Speaking of the incident in 2001 when Ian Bailey had assaulted her with crutches, she said that his Achilles tendon had snapped, 'It is meant to be one of the most painful things on earth. He was on strong painkillers and had taken alcohol that night. His resistance was low to anything I would say at that time,' she explained. She admitted that she had made a complaint to Gardaí, but said, 'I was put under enormous pressure. Two detectives came around to the house. The Gardaí seemed absolutely delighted. They were revelling in it.'

Ms Thomas maintained that the amount of publicity the assault received was completely out of proportion for a domestic incident. She pointed out that while 10,000 cases of domestic violence are reported each year, more than twice that number are never even reported to Gardaí.

Jules Thomas said that she remains very angry over the manner of her and Ian Bailey's arrest in 1997. 'I couldn't speak. I felt so damaged,' she claimed. As Gardaí approached her home, with Ian Bailey under arrest in the squad car, 'It was like the ground fell away from under my feet. I was absolutely stunned. I just said to them that that they were making a big mistake.'

Ms Thomas described the questioning at Bandon Garda Station as incredibly intensive. 'Having three detectives question you at the one time just fries your brains. I just couldn't speak after it all,' she maintained.

DAY SEVEN – Tuesday, 16 December

The seventh day of the hearing opened to a packed court-room. Shoppers, old-age pensioners, and even parents attending the nearby Christmas pantomime in Cork's Opera House vied with barristers and solicitors to view what had become the most sensational show in town.

This was undoubtedly the most traumatic day for Ian

Bailey, a day of damaging evidence that saw three witnesses – Ritchie and Rosie Shelly and Malachi Reed – insist that he confessed the killing of Sophie Toscan du Plantier to them. Others painted a stark picture of Ian Bailey as an eccentric character with strange hobbies and bizarre behaviour. From the testimony of neighbours, former workmates and friends a remarkable portrait emerged.

A total of twenty independent witnesses began their testimony – fourteen on day seven alone. They variously and flatly contradicted Ian Bailey's version of events. They also painted a graphic picture of the freelance reporter, poet, New Age gardener, bodhrán player and woodcarver.

The most devastating evidence about Ian Bailey came from the Shellys and Malachi Reed. Ritchie and Rosie Shelly were invited to the home of Ian Bailey and Jules Thomas on New Year's Eve 1998 – and were left so terrified by Ian Bailey's comments and actions that they insisted on departing early.

Ritchie Shelly told Judge Moran that he and his wife had met Jules Thomas and Ian Bailey in a local pub and were invited back to Liscaha, having been told that a number of other couples would be coming. In the end, they were surprised to find that they were the only guests. Ian Bailey had dominated the evening with talk about the murder of Sophie Toscan du Plantier and had insisted on showing the Shellys his case file. After Mr Shelly realised that his wife felt very uncomfortable and wanted to go home, he rang his father and asked him to pick them up. Then, Ian Bailey came back into the room.

'He [Ian] came back into the kitchen and he seemed very upset. He was crying and put his arms around me and said, "I did it, I did it". I asked him "you did what?" And he said, "I went too far." I assumed he was talking about the murder because that's what we were talking about all night,' Mr Shelly claimed. The next day, Mr Shelly said he met Ian Bailey in a Schull pub and told him that he was now convinced that he was the murderer.

Rosie Shelly gave evidence that the incident left her very frightened. 'He seemed to be obsessed by it [the murder]. I think he had every article that was published in his file,' she said. After witnessing Ian Bailey's emotional outburst, she insisted to her husband that they leave the house without waiting for their lift. 'I immediately recognised that it was a kind of confession,' she declared.

Mirroring that evidence, Malachi Reed testified that when he got a lift home from Schull with Ian Bailey as a fourteen-year-old schoolboy, the freelance reporter had also confessed the killing to him. Mr Reed (now twenty-one) recalled how Ian Bailey said to him, 'It was fine up until I went up and bashed her f***ing brains in.' Mr Reed remembered his reaction: 'I got a very cold shiver, nervousness. I didn't know what to do. I kept my mouth shut for two miles. He said, "How are you getting on in school?" I said the first thing that came into my head.' Malachi, who was friendly at the time with Funella Thomas, a daughter of Jules Thomas, said that Ian Bailey, who had been drinking, seemed agitated and upset when they began their journey.

He said that he didn't tell his mother about the incident until the following day. 'I tried to put it out of my mind as best I could,' he declared. When he did tell his mother what had happened, they were both so frightened that they put dead bolts on all their doors. 'I then avoided him as best I could,' Mr Reed added. He agreed that he now doesn't like Ian Bailey very much: 'As much as you'd like anyone who admitted to murdering a woman.'

Rejecting suggestions by the plaintiff's barrister, Jim Duggan, that his story was 'rubbish', Mr Reed said, 'It's not rubbish. It's the truth. I have no reason to lie.' When asked why he had accepted a lift from Mr Bailey on two subsequent occasions, Malachi Reed replied, 'Because I didn't have the opportunity to jump over the ditch.'

His mother, Irene Amanda Reed, confirmed to Paul Gallagher that her son was 'very agitated and very upset' when he told her what Mr Bailey had said to him. 'You can imagine how you would feel after an incident like this. I was absolutely terrified. I put the locks on every single night,' she declared. Mrs Reed also dismissed suggestions from Jim Duggan that her son could have made a mistake and confused his story. 'I don't think so. He was definite and he was absolutely terrified. And my son is not a liar,' she insisted to the court. She added that the possibility of such comments being made by Ian Bailey to a fourteen-year-old boy did not surprise her. 'Mr Bailey has always seemed to do quite unusual things. He is quite an unusual person,' she declared.

Examples of exactly how unusual a man Ian Bailey was were provided by a number of other witnesses. One former neighbour, Brian Jackson, described Ian Bailey as 'a strange, bohemian kind of character'. 'Everybody said he was a strange man,' he elaborated. 'I heard that his hobby was destroying religious artefacts. He had a reputation for walk-ing at night with his "thinking" stick. It was a big branch of a stick … [he would] mostly go out at night or in the early morning.' Mr Jackson also said that after Ian Bailey paid a visit to his house, a family member told him that Ian Bailey had been smoking a joint. 'We opened it up and it had this green stuff inside it,' he claimed. Brian Jackson also alleged that Ian Bailey had been tending a bonfire on the Liscaha property on St Stephen's Day 1996.

This evidence was supported by another neighbour, Louise Kennedy, who was adamant that there had been a fire on the property of Jules Thomas and Ian Bailey on 26 December. Throughout the hearing, Ian Bailey denied this claim and said that the allegation, which had also appeared in some of the newspapers, clearly suggested he was trying to destroy possible evidence.

Another witness, Caroline Leftwick, claimed that when she spoke to Ian Bailey on 23 December 1996 he had seemed 'very excited' at being able to cover the Sophie Toscan du Plantier murder for some newspapers. She also maintained that Jules Thomas had told her at a party that Sophie's body was in a terrible state. 'Jules came and sat close to me in the corner. I can't remember her exact words. But she said that the body had been a terrible sight.'

Ceri Williams told the Court that she felt that Ian Bailey could be 'very intimidating' at times. She said that while Ian Bailey was very intelligent, he was also known for being quite eccentric. 'I don't like him,' she said. 'I don't agree with the beating of women. In fact, I don't agree with the beating of anyone.' 'It [the assault on Jules Thomas] was so brutal I did not want someone who was capable of that to be near my children,' she added. Ms Williams also claimed that, in late January 1997, before Ian Bailey's first arrest by Gardaí, one local woman, Diane Martin, had already told him to his face at a party that he was a murderer. 'He said nothing at all,' she declared.

In a critical piece of evidence, Alfie Lyons – Sophie's next-door-neighbour in Toormore – said that Ian Bailey had met Sophie Toscan du Plantier some eighteen months before her murder. Ian Bailey had insisted throughout the defamation action that he had not met the Frenchwoman and was never introduced to her. But Alfie Lyons recalled that he had personally introduced Bailey to Ms du Plantier when she called to his house in June 1995. Ian Bailey had been doing some gardening work for Mr Lyons when Sophie called around to say hello. 'As far as I can recollect, I did introduce him to Sophie Toscan du Plantier. I am 90% certain that I did,' Mr Lyons declared.

Veteran British journalist, Paul Webster, also told the court that Ian Bailey gave him to understand that he knew Sophie Toscan du Plantier. Mr Webster – who was based in Paris during 1996/97, working for the *Guardian* – revealed that Ian Bailey contacted him about reporting on the West Cork murder. Bailey said that he was in a good position to assist with information on the story. 'He made it absolutely clear that he had talked to her – before, there is no doubt about that at all – and seen her on the day she died,' Mr Webster declared.

Another witness flatly contradicted Ian Bailey's version of how he arrived at the murder scene on 23 December. Shirley Foster – the woman who found Sophie's battered body – remained adamant that she met Ian Bailey that lunchtime as he drove up her laneway at speed, and not on the open roadway, as he had claimed. She said that Ian Bailey seemed in quite a hurry as he drove up the laneway, which led to only three houses, including hers and that of

Ms Toscan du Plantier.

Provision freelance photographic agency boss Mike MacSweeney insisted that Ian Bailey told him that pictures of the murder scene were taken around 11am on 23 December, over two hours before Mr Bailey claimed he first heard of the murder. Earlier, journalist Eddie Cassidy, the West Cork correspondent with the *Cork Examiner*, denied that he had told Ian Bailey at 1.40pm on 23 December that a murder had been committed which involved a French national. Mr Cassidy said that at the time he rang Ian Bailey he was not aware of the nationality of the deceased or that it was a murder; he thought the remains might have been the result of a hit-and-run accident, possibly with a member of a local New Age Traveller encampment. In her testimony, Caroline Leftwick had said that in a phone call before midday on 23 December, Ian Bailey had told her that a French woman who was on holiday had been killed.

Another witness, James Camier, testified that Jules Thomas called to his vegetable stall in Goleen before 11 am on 23 December and told him about the murder. Ms Thomas had said that this was impossible and that she actually went to Goleen on Christmas Eve, twenty-four hours later. However, James Camier was adamant about the date – and that Jules Thomas not only told him there had been a murder but that the victim was a French national. 'I'm here on oath, your worship, and I say she did,' Mr Camier declared. Denying that there was any question of his statement being made under duress, Mr Camier said, 'I take my own decisions and on my own conscience. I would stress the statement I made was off my own mind and my own conscience.'

DAY EIGHT – Wednesday, 17 December

The eighth day of the hearing was marked by yet another revelation in a case already full of surprises, and by the most graphic account yet of the violence perpetrated against Jules Thomas. The opening witness was Schull shopkeeper Marie Farrell, who delivered arguably the most gripping testimony of the entire hearing.

The soft-spoken West Cork shopkeeper told the court that she had received a threatening phone call from an anonymous woman forty-eight hours before she was due to testify, warning her to 'keep my bloody mouth shut'. Mrs Farrell admitted she was a reluctant witness and was only appearing because of a subpoena served on behalf of the newspapers. Then, slowly but convincingly she described how Ian Bailey had been 'torturing' her and had made her life 'a living nightmare' in a determined campaign to force her to retract a statement she had made to the Gardaí about the Sophie Toscan du Plantier murder. Mrs Farrell insisted to Paul Gallagher that, just as she had told Gardaí in that statement, she saw Ian Bailey in the early hours of 23

December 1996 close to Sophie Toscan du Plantier's home. (Mr Bailey had sworn to Judge Moran that he never left the home of his partner, Jules Thomas, on that date, and that, after getting out of bed in the early hours of the morning, he had spent the night writing).

She told the court that she had been living in fear of Ian Bailey. 'I ended up in debt because I was so afraid to stay there [her shop]) because of Ian Bailey. I was afraid to let my children out because of him. It was awful,' she declared. When she had first noticed the 'tall man, in a dark coat, kind of distinctive looking' in Schull she didn't know who he was. In the early hours of 23 December, she saw the same man not far from Sophie Toscan du Plantier's home – swinging his arms and walking along the road in a very distinctive fashion. It was sometime in January 1997 when she saw the man again in a local newsagents and he was identified to her as Ian Bailey. She immediately informed the Gardaí of what she had seen.

A short time later, Mrs Farrell claimed, she was told by Jules Thomas that Ian Bailey wanted to meet her. On another occasion, Jules Thomas invited her to her home so that she could record a statement claiming the Gardaí wanted her to make a false declaration. The witness said that Jules Thomas told her they must do everything possible to protect Ian.

'I was told that we had to meet and that there were things

we would have to discuss. He said "I am being set up by detectives".' Ian Bailey then called to her knitwear and ice cream shop, opened his coat and said to her, 'I am all wired up'. 'He had a tape recorder,' she explained, 'And he wanted me to say that that the Gardaí were forcing me to make a false statement.' While in the shop, Ian Bailey stood on a chair and swung his arms about, asking was her shop clean. Mrs Farrell initially thought that he was referring to hygiene but then realised that he was talking about 'bugs' or electronic listening devices.

She said she felt very nervous being alone in the shop with Mr Bailey. She noticed how wide his arm span was and said she immediately thought: 'He could kill me in two minutes and the Gardaí are away up the street.' She said she was stunned when Mr Bailey proceeded to produce her partner's address in London – and then addresses where she had formerly lived in her native Longford.

When Mrs Farrell refused to make the statement and failed to contact Mr Bailey within a time frame he had specified, she suddenly noticed a change in his behaviour. He came into her shop and said he knew things about her. 'He said if I scratched his back, he would scratch mine,' she declared. The witness told the court that at one point Ian Bailey shouted at her: 'I know you saw me ... but I did not kill Sophie.'

Mrs Farrell said that Ian Bailey would then make

cutthroat gestures to her every time they met – and would point his extended finger at his temple in an execution-style move. She also started to receive threatening phone calls. She was so scared that she hired three extra staff so she would never be left in her shop alone.

In cross-examination by Jim Duggan for the plaintiff, Mrs Farrell vehemently denied inviting Ian Bailey to her shop. 'I don't think any woman in her right frame of mind would invite Ian Bailey to her shop, especially when she is on her own,' Mrs Farrell declared. 'It's a well known fact that he is abusive towards women.' She also denied being put under any duress by the Gardaí to make a statement about what she saw in the early hours of 23 December 1996 on the Schull to Goleen road. 'The Gardaí didn't know me from Adam until I contacted them,' she asserted.

When Marie Farrell concluded her evidence, brief testimony was then taken from three witnesses: *Irish Independent* pictures editor Padraig Beirne and West Cork musician Paul O'Colmain, who both gave evidence about contacts with Mr Bailey over Christmas 1996, while Garda Supt. Vincent Duggan gave testimony about investigating the complaints made by Marie Farrell about Ian Bailey.

Ironically, both of the witnesses who gave evidence in the afternoon were once friends of Ian Bailey. Peter Bielecki and Bill Fuller had been asked by Judge Moran to remain outside the courtroom on earlier days because of claims by

Mr Bailey of alleged intimidation.

Mr Bielecki told how he was called to Jules Thomas's house in May 1996 by her distraught daughter, Virginia, after Ian Bailey had assaulted her mother. 'It was absolutely the most appalling thing I have ever witnessed,' Mr Bielecki declared. 'Jules Thomas was curled up in a foetal position at the foot of the bed. I could hear what I can only describe as almost animal sounds. It was as if someone had their soul ripped out.'

Peter Bielecki struggled to control his emotions as he remembered the incident. 'I am sorry, this is very distressing.'

He went on to say that he saw clumps of Jules Thomas's hair torn out, bite marks on her hands, scratches and bruises to her face and her eye swollen to an enormous size. He said that her eye was so damaged that a pink-coloured fluid was dripping from it, which he presumed must have been antibodies. Mr Bielecki – who lived near the family – then agreed to a request by Virginia to drive her mother to a hospital in Cork for medical treatment.

He also agreed to stay over at the Thomas household that night – 'because Ian Bailey was still in close proximity. I think I stayed for about three weeks in the house.' He revealed that he slept on a sofa on the ground floor with a hammer under his pillow, given to him by Jules Thomas's daughters, just in case Mr Bailey ever attempted to return to the house. 'He is a rather large man and I'm not so sure I could have handled him,' Peter Bielecki explained. From that moment, he told Judge Patrick Moran, his friendship with Ian Bailey was over.

The court heard that the two men had become close friends in the early 1990s through their common love of Irish traditional music. But after this incident Mr Bielecki 'felt betrayed by Ian. I thought that I was a good judge of character. Obviously I wasn't. From the moment that Mr Bailey did what he did to Jules Thomas, I no longer considered him worthy of my friendship in any shape or form,' he declared.

Jules Thomas sat in the courtroom throughout Peter Bielecki's harrowing account of her ordeal, showing no reaction to what she heard.

Another former friend and workmate of Ian Bailey, Bill Fuller, denied that he had tried to intimidate Ian Bailey during the hearing. Mr Fuller apologised to the court and to Mr Bailey for having spoken to him outside the courtroom during the case. Ian Bailey had claimed that his former work colleague said to him: 'I've got you now.' Mr Fuller stated that his actual words were: 'You have sweat on your brow'.

In his evidence, Mr Fuller said that Ian Bailey had made a strange comment to him, speaking in the second person, (as other witnesses had testified Mr Bailey was wont to do) about the killing of Sophie Toscan du Plantier. He said: 'You did it. You killed Sophie. You did it, you saw her in

Spar on Saturday; you saw her walking up the aisle with her tight arse. You fancied her. You went up to see what you could get. She ran away screaming. You chased her. You went too far, you had to finish her off.'

The witness said he then commented to Mr Bailey: 'Sounds like something you would say.' Ian Bailey replied: 'Funny you should say that, that is how I met Jules. I saw her tight arse. But she let me in.' After the conversation, Mr Fuller said he was quite shocked and upset. 'I was very disturbed and I was quite afraid.' He also told the court how a neighbour of Mr Bailey's had reported hearing screams late one evening, and was convinced that the screams were not from a fox or another wild animal.

And, suddenly, it was over. It emerged that Bill Fuller was to be the last witness called by the newspapers. The case that some reporters had been confidently predicting would last into the New Year was finished. Judge Moran was informed that none of the journalists involved in the articles complained of would be called, and that the defence were ready for their final submissions.

DAYS NINE and TEN – Thursday, 18 December and Friday, 19 December
In his closing submission for the defence, Paul Gallagher SC, accused Ian Bailey of misleading Cork Circuit Civil Court by telling 'lie upon lie upon lie' during the hearing.

'A person has a right to reputation but no person has a right to come to court to tell lie after lie after lie,' he said.

In a summation that took almost five hours, the Senior Counsel detailed how Ian Bailey's evidence to the hearing was flatly contradicted in numerous ways by independent witnesses. He also contended that Ian Bailey tried to mislead the court in relation to the nature of the violence against Ms Thomas. Referring to the testimony of Marie Farrell, Malachi Reed, the Shellys, Alfie Lyons and Peter Bielecki, among others, he said, 'These witnesses establish the truth of matters that Mr Bailey said were lies'.

Mr Gallagher maintained that Ian Bailey was a violent man – and the abuse to which he subjected his partner, Jules Thomas, was nothing short of horrific. 'It is patently ludicrous to suggest that damages should be paid to a man who complains of being defamed by being called violent when that is clearly what he is,' the Senior Counsel argued.

Ian Bailey's barrister, Jim Duggan, claimed that the newspapers being sued had published articles which 'said to the man who read them that this man murdered Sophie Toscan du Plantier. It is an allegation of murder most foul.' He was therefore 'flabbergasted that the defendants finished their evidence without calling one journalist relevant to the articles – no writer, no editor.'

'I was deprived of trying to ascertain from them how the background of these articles came to be written,' Mr

Duggan complained. Ian Bailey had been subjected to 'trial by ambush'.

Jim Duggan also told the court that the newspapers had failed to offer any evidence whatsoever on some specific allegations printed about Mr Bailey in the offending articles, for example that he had been violent towards his ex-wife, and that he had been burning clothes on 26 December 1996.

In classic libel hearing fashion, he finished with a quotation about the media from Stanley Baldwin on the exercise of power without responsibility: 'The proposition of these papers is aiming at power and power without responsibility. The perogative of the harlot throughout the ages'.

The two-day summation effectively ended any hopes of a ruling being delivered before Christmas – much to the relief of the exhausted local media corps. Judge Moran, amid initial speculation that he could deliver his ruling on the Monday following the end of the hearing, advised that given the huge volume of material and transcripts to be reviewed, he would now consider the matter over Christmas. He set 9 January 2004 as the date when he would deliver his judgement.

However, within three days that date had been postponed once again because of the requirement to handle other business on the Circuit Court list. The new judgement date would be Monday, 19 January – leaving both sides over three weeks to await their fate.

The Ruling – Monday, 19 January 2004

Cork Circuit Court was the focus of a media posse never seen before outside a Cork courtroom. From 7am, TV crews thronged Camden Quay. RTÉ, TV3 and TG4 were joined by crews from Sky TV and even from France. Such was the gathering of TV crews, radio reporters and photographers that minor traffic delays resulted as curious motorists slowed down to find out what was going on.

Local reporters, aware that seats would be at a premium, slipped into the building at 9am. Public interest in the decision was running at fever pitch. Cork radio stations County Sound/96FM and Red FM ran hourly news bulletins building up to the verdict. By 10am, when the doors finally opened, there was a scramble for seats as almost 200 people tried to pack themselves into Courtroom No. 1 for Judge Moran's decision. Many reporters from France and England – taken by surprise at the extent of the crowd – ended up taking their notes while standing in a crush at the rear of the courtroom.

For the first time since the hearing started, Ian Bailey was not accompanied by Jules Thomas. It subsequently transpired that the Welsh artist was suffering from a cold and was too ill to attend court. It was perhaps just as well.

Confounding predictions that the judgement could take several hours to deliver, it was completed in less than forty minutes – and Ian Bailey's bid to clear his name had been left in ruins. In a devastating ruling, Judge Moran accepted that the British-born reporter had tried to mislead the hearing, that he was a violent man and that none of the eight newspapers had defamed him by referring to him as the prime suspect in the Sophie Toscan du Plantier murder investigation.

In a sweeping rejection of Ian Bailey's claims, Judge Moran struck out the defamation actions taken against the *Sunday Independent*, the *Independent on Sunday*, the *Daily Telegraph*, the *Times*, the *Sunday Times* and the *Irish Star*. However, he ruled that, in relation to the remaining two actions, Mr Bailey had been defamed by both the *Irish Mirror* and the *Irish Sun* on a subsidiary issue to the main complaint. He found that no evidence had been offered on an allegation published by both papers that the Manchester-born journalist had committed violence against his ex-wife, Sara Limbrick.

In reference to the overall complaint of defamation, Judge Moran said he was satisfied that the newspaper's defence of justification was entirely correct and fully established. The newspaper coverage did not identify Mr Bailey as the murderer; the articles had correctly identified Ian Bailey as a suspect in the case and they had also reported his assertions that he had nothing to do with the murder. He pointed out that a number of issues had not been directly proven by the defendants – amongst them a claim that Mr

Bailey was seen burning clothing and that he had been violent towards his ex-wife, Sara Limbrick. Judge Moran held that the claim of violence towards his ex-wife had been defamatory and he awarded damages to Mr Bailey against both the *Irish Sun* and the *Irish Mirror*, the two newspapers who had published the claim. He awarded total damages of €8,000 – to be divided as €4,000 against each of the two titles.

Judge Moran then singled out inconsistencies between evidence given during the hearing by Mr Bailey and that offered by twenty independent witnesses. He stated that, on the balance of probabilities, he accepted the evidence of the newspaper witnesses. He accepted evidence from Marie Farrell that Ian Bailey had been on the Schull-Goleen road in the early hours of 23 December 1996 – despite the plaintiff's assertion that he never left Jules Thomas's home. He also accepted the evidence of Malachi Reed and Ritchie and Rosie Shelly that Ian Bailey had admitted the killing to them.

'I accept what Mr and Mrs Shelly tell me – and that he [Ian Bailey] did say that,' the judge announced. He also said that he accepted the evidence of Malachi Reed, who had claimed that Mr Bailey told him he had 'smashed her brains in'. 'I think this was a form of bravado on Mr Bailey's part … trying to impress a fourteen-year-old boy,' he declared.

Judge Moran also accepted evidence from Alfie Lyons that Ian Bailey had been introduced to Sophie Toscan du

Plantier – despite the plaintiff insisting that he never met her. However, he conceded that while it was likely the two may have met, they did not really know each other.

He accepted evidence from two witnesses – Louise Kennedy and Brian Jackson – that Mr Bailey had been tending a fire on 26 December 1996.

But in delivering his ruling, Judge Moran repeated his warning that the libel hearing was not a murder trial. 'I was anxious that this hearing should not take on the mantle of a murder trial. I am afraid that one or two times it did and I am sorry it did.' Furthermore, he advised that, as a civil action, a different standard of proof was involved – and matters could be taken 'on the balance of probabilities' rather than as beyond a reasonable doubt. Had this been a criminal matter, he said, it was likely that some of the witnesses would have been ruled as inadmissable.

In commenting on the overall case, Judge Moran said he was struck by the coolness of Ian Bailey in the witness box. 'The thing that occurred to me was that he was a very cool witness. He never got annoyed during the lengthy and protracted cross-examination. The only time he showed any discomfort was when he was making a complaint about something that happened to him within the walls of this building.'

Judge Moran felt that when Jules Thomas was giving evidence about the 'nasty' assaults she suffered at Ian

Bailey's hands, she tried to 'push it under the carpet' through minimising the nature of the attacks.

Pointing out that the plaintiff was fond of notoriety and capable of self-publicity, Judge Moran remarked on the fact that, within twenty-four hours of Mr Bailey's first arrest by Gardaí in relation to the murder on 10 February 1997, he had conducted two interviews with RTÉ, one on the Pat Kenny Show. He later went on to grant interviews to news-papers – and even posed for photographs.

'To me, this was quite unusual for someone who had been arrested on suspicion of a serious charge. Normally people withdraw into the background following their release from custody,' the judge commented. 'But Mr Bailey did not; he gave interviews. One can only presume Mr Bailey is a man who likes a certain amount of notoriety, likes to be in the limelight and likes a bit of self publicity.'

In relation to Mr Bailey's arrest by Gardaí in February 1997, Judge Moran emphasised that officers only take such steps with good reason. 'When Gardaí make an arrest for serious criminal offences, particularly murder, they usually do so for very good reasons and have a strong suspicion of involvement …' he declared.

In reference to Mr Bailey's objection to the newspapers referring to him as a violent man, Judge Moran delivered what was perhaps the kernel of his judgement. 'I would have no hesitation in describing Mr Bailey as a violent man,' he declared. 'The defendants were perfectly justified in describing him as violent towards women – he has not been defamed by that,' Judge Moran added.

The British-born reporter looked shocked and furious at the ruling. At one point, as Judge Moran was rejecting claim after claim, Ian Bailey leaned forward, closed his eyes and appeared to try to meditate.

A hearing on costs in the case was scheduled for Thursday, 12 February.

Thus began what Jim Duggan BL was later to complain of as 'open season on Ian Bailey'. A mêlée erupted as he left the courthouse following the devastating judgement. Escorted by three Gardaí, the journalist had to fight his way to his waiting taxi through a scrum of reporters, photographers and TV crews. Every question shouted at him was studiously ignored.

Awarding of Costs – Thursday, 12 February

For the only time in the entire action, Ian Bailey opted not to attend the 12 February costs ruling – a decision which was probably wise in light of the overwhelming financial consequences for him. And, for the first time in the hearing, there was a sparse attendance, with most observers already predicting the worst possible outcome for Ian Bailey.

Judge Moran ruled that Ian Bailey was to pay three-fifths of the costs of the six newspapers that successfully defended his defamation action. Mr Bailey's legal team were also awarded only half their costs – around €29,000 – against two other newspapers (*Irish Sun* and *Irish Mirror*), which were found to have defamed the Manchester-born reporter. The total cost of the libel action was now estimated at €650,000 – €450,000 for the eight newspapers and €200,000 for the plaintiff.

Judge Moran's ruling meant that Ian Bailey was liable for over €200,000 of the newspapers' €450,000 costs. The €250,000 balance would have to be paid by the newspapers.

The balance of the plaintiff's legal costs – €170,000 – remained the focus of talks between Mr Bailey and his legal team. Judge Moran said he was reducing the costs imposed on Mr Bailey – three-fifths of the actions successfully defended – because the newspapers had used four separate solicitor firms and had not pooled resources sufficiently.

The newspapers' costs included substantial witness expenses, with over fifty people having being served with subpoenas – and a number having to be accommodated in Cork hotels pending their testimony at the hearing.

In delivering his costs ruling, Judge Moran endorsed complaints by the newspapers' counsel, Paul Gallagher SC, that the plaintiff had misled the Court during the sensational ten-day hearing. Judge Moran also dismissed complaints from Mr Bailey's counsel, Jim Duggan BL, that the action had degenerated into 'trial by ambush' through blatant collusion between the Gardaí and the newspapers.

All eight newspapers sought a receiver motion, which will freeze the €8,000 award against the *Irish Mirror* and *Irish Sun* until such time as Mr Bailey clarifies how he intends to pay the €200,000 legal costs. If he is unable to pay the fees, his €8,000 award will then be the focus of a confiscation motion by the newspapers. It is thought highly unlikely that Mr Bailey will be able to make any significant contribution to the hearing costs. The forty-six-year-old owns or controls no major assets in Ireland – and legal experts were of the opinion that the newspapers will proba-bly have to foot all their own costs and the partial costs award granted Mr Bailey's legal team. Mr Bailey's partner, Jules Thomas, confirmed that he had no way of paying the costs, and was 'a man of straw'.

But Independent Newspapers' managing director Michael Roche confirmed that the group will be vigorously pursuing its costs. Just two weeks later, Ian Bailey took the decision to lodge papers signalling a High Court appeal against the six newspapers who had triumphed against him. Those newspapers, in turn, all lodged papers appealing against Judge Moran's decision to award them only partial costs.

Hugh Hannigan, solicitor with McAleese & Co., which represents Independent Newspapers, amongst others, felt that the High Court appeal was yet another gamble by Ian

Bailey. 'Mr Bailey had nothing to lose by taking a gamble with a libel action in the Circuit Court and now he has nothing to lose by taking another gamble in the High Court,' he commented. Mr Hannigan pointed out that Mr Bailey doesn't have to lodge any money in court as a preliminary to his High Court action.

However, Jules Thomas defended the appeal as inevitable given the 'horrendous and awful nature of the articles'. 'No, we are not sore losers, but justice was not served. It was very unfair. That's what this is all about,' she declared. Ms Thomas also insisted that the revelations about the domestic abuse she suffered at Ian Bailey's hands were not a factor in the appeal. 'It makes no difference to me – it's out there. What's the difference about it a second time around? I know it's a bit like a public confessional but it doesn't make any difference to me inside,' she said.

The Welsh artist also insisted that the decision to appeal was proof of Ian Bailey's innocence – and of his determination to clear his name. 'Would a guilty person honestly put themselves through this twice?' she asked. 'He was defamed. The articles were absolute, pure lies. It was fabrication by journalists going over the top. I mean, it makes you feel outraged. If it happened to you, you would do the same.'

If a High Court appeal does go ahead it is unlikely to be heard until mid 2005 or even 2006.

POSTSCRIPT

In the aftermath of the sensational judgement, Ian Bailey left the Liscaha home he shared with Jules Thomas and, for almost two months, played a game of cat-and-mouse with the media who were determined to track him down for comment on the legal action. Then, in late March, 2004 Ian Bailey re-appeared in Schull and resumed his life with Jules Thomas. In March, he also began signing on for Social Welfare. He has since declined all requests for interviews. He continues his hobby of wood-carving and has also been preparing a series of articles on wildlife in the West Cork area.

* * *

In December 2002, the Toscan du Plantier/Bouniol family filed a civil suit against Ian Bailey. However, Sophie's husband, Daniel Toscan du Plantier, who had been instrumental in initiating the case, died suddenly in March 2003 as he attended the Berlin Film Festival. The action is being pursued by Sophie's parents, Georges and Marguerite Bouniol and her son, Pierre Louis.

Ian Bailey has appointed Cork solicitor, Frank Buttimer, who runs one of Munster's largest and most successful legal practices, to handle the action on his behalf.

BIBLIOGRAPHY

Baden, Dr Michael and Roach, Marion, *Dead Reckoning, (Arrow Books,* 2001)

Britton, Paul, *The Jigsaw Man*, (Corgi Books, 1998)

Capote, Truman, *In Cold Blood*, (Penguin Classics, 2000)

Fitzgerald, F Scott, *Tender Is The Night*, (Penguin Books, 1986)

Lee, Henry C. and Harris, Howard A., *Physical Evidence in Forensic Science*, (Tucson, AZ Lawyers And Judges Publishing Company, 2000)

Masters, Brian, *Killing For Company*, (Jonathan Cape, 1985)

Large, Peter Somerville, *The Coast Of West Cork,* (Appletree Press, 1985)

Wassell, Elizabeth, *The Thing He Loves*, (Brandon Books, 2001)

Wilson, Colin and Seaman, Donald, *Encyclopaedia of Modern Murder*, (Pan Books, 1989)

Wilson, Colin and Seaman, Donald, *The Serial Killers*, (Virgin Books, 1996)

'Whose Body of Evidence?', The Economist 348, July 1, 1998.

Forensic Art: Little Known, Highly Effective. Wesley Neville, Florence County Sheriff's Office www.fcso.org

DNA Databanks, Giving Police A Powerful Weapon, and Critics, *New York Times*, 1998.

'Crime Scene Investigation', Katherine Ramsland, Internet.

'Stalkers; The Pyschological Terrorist', Katherine Ramsland, Internet.

FBI certifies DNA evidence, Reuters, 1997.

Newspapers: *The Examiner, The Sunday Independent, The Sunday Tribune, The Star, the Irish Mirror, The Sun, The Sunday World, The News Of The World, The Irish Times, The Irish Independent, Le Figaro, Paris Match, Le Monde.*

Television: RTÉ news bulletins. 'Crimeline' reconstruction, January 1997.

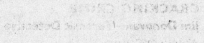

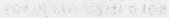

MORE **TRUE CRIME** FROM
THE O'BRIEN PRESS

CRACKING CRIME
Jim Donovan – Forensic Detective
Niamh O'Connor

Dr Jim Donovan, the State Forensic Scientist, was the victim of a car bomb planted by The General *aka* Martin Cahill. Refusing to bow to Cahill's threats, he went on to work on some of the biggest cases the country has witnessed, including the shooting of Garda Reynolds by Noel and Marie Murray, the assassination of Lord Mountbatten and British Ambassador Christopher Ewart Biggs by the IRA, the abduction, torture and murder of Mary Duffy. This is a rare and compelling insight into the gruelling but important work of the forensic scientist.

Paperback €10.95/STG£7.99

SOLD INTO MARRIAGE
Sean Boyne

In 1973 a sixteen-year-old Irish schoolgirl was sold into marriage by her father. Her groom was a farmer almost four times her age. Despite a pre-nuptial agreement guaranteeing that there would be no sex, her husband raped and beat her repeatedly. She made desperate pleas for help, but the legal system, the police and the clergy failed her. This is the heartbreaking story of a young girl whose life was ruined by her own father, who gave her away in exchange for money, a Morris Mini and the promise of land.

Paperback €9.95/STG£6.99

THE BLACK WIDOW
Niamh O'Connor

The best-selling story of Catherine Nevin, the woman who wanted it all and was willing to kill to get it.

When Tom Nevin was brutally murdered, none seemed as grief-stricken as his widow, Catherine. She stood by the graveside holding a single red rose: the classic symbol of a lost love. But there was a lot more to Catherine Nevin than met the eye. Four years later she stood in the dock, accused of murdering her husband. The trial kept the country enthralled, as every day more bizarre stories emerged: contract killers, money laundering, the IRA, sexual affairs. An incredible story of a cold, calculating woman and her desire for money, power and prestige.

Paperback €9.95/STG£6.99

HOSTAGE
Notorious Irish Kidnappings
Paul Howard

Inside accounts of Ireland's most famous abduction cases. **SHERGAR** – full transcripts of the negotiations for the Epsom Derby winner; **BEN DUNNE** – Fr Dermod McCarthy tells the astonishing story of his meeting with the IRA in his bid to release the supermarket supremo; **TIEDE HERREMA** – how he built up a relationship with his kidnapper, Eddie Gallaghe, and his bitterness at the deal that was not honoured; **DON TIDEY** – An IRA source reveals doubts about the kidnapping and the price the organisation paid for its failure; **LORD & LADY DONOUGHMORE** – the peer's unpublished diary of the kidnap ordeal.

Paperback €10.95/STG£7.99

BREAK-OUT!
Famous Prison Escapes
Paddy Hayes

The bizarre, daring and sometimes farcical true stories of Ireland's jailbreakers.

In 1942 German spy Gunter Schutz ordered his escape costume from Mountjoy's unsuspecting Governor; in 1943 twenty-one men broke out of Derry prison and emerged in a coal shed; the 'Magnificent Seven' swan to freedom from the prison ship *Maidstone* in 1972 after a seal showed them the way; in 1973 three prisoners were scooped by helicopter from the exercise yard of Mountjoy in broad daylight; in 1974 Kenneth Littlejohn managed to squeeze through his cell bars after going on hunger strike; in 1983 a breakout from the high security H Blocks involved an incredible thirty-eight prisoners.

Paperback €10.95/STG£7.99

THE GENERAL
Godfather of Crime
Paul Williams

In a twenty-year career marked by obsessive secrecy, brutality and meticulous planning, Martin Cahill, aka The General, netted over £40 million. He was untouchable – until a bullet from an IRA hitman ended it all. A compelling read, this book reveals Cahill's bizarre personality and the activities of the Tango Squad – the special police unit that targeted him using tactics employed against the infamous Kray Gang.

Paperback €10.95/STG£7.99

GANGLAND
Paul Williams

A chilling read, *Gangland* gives the inside story on a dark and sinister world. Who are the families that form the Irish mafia? What have been their most daring exploits? How do they hide their activities from the authorities? Williams examines the way in which they have spread their net across the country and beyond, reaping huge profits which allow them to live the high life while bringing misery to others.

Paperback €9.95/STG£6.99

Send for our full-colour catalogue

ORDER FORM

Please send me the books as marked.

I enclose cheque/postal order for € . . . .

(please add €1.50/STG£1.00 P&P per title)

OR please charge my credit card ☐ Access/Mastercard ☐ Visa

Card Number _ _ _ _ _   _ _ _ _ _   _ _ _ _ _   _ _ _ _ _

Expiry Date _ _ _ / _ _ _

Name. . . . . Tel. . . . .

Address . . . .

. . . .

Please send orders to: THE O'BRIEN PRESS, 20 Victoria Road, Dublin 6, Ireland.

Tel: +353 1 4923333; Fax: + 353 1 4922777; E-mail: books@obrien.ie

Website: www.obrien.ie

Note: prices are subject to change without notice